D1599085

Titanic Lessons in Project Leadership

Effective Communication and Team Building

by Ranjit Sidhu

LIBRARY
NSCC - STRAIT AREA CAMPUS
226 REEVES ST.
PORT HAWKESBURY NS
B9A 2A2 CANADA

First Edition

Multi-Media
Publications Inc.

Oshawa, Ontario

Titanic Lessons in Project Leadership:
Effective Communication and Team Building
by Ranjit Sidhu

Managing Editor:	Kevin Aguanno
Series Editor:	Mark Kozak-Holland
Copy Editor:	Susan Andres
Typesetting:	Peggy LeTrent and Kevin Aguanno
Cover Design:	Kevin Aguanno
eBook Conversion:	Charles Sin

Published by:
Multi-Media Publications Inc.
Box 58043, Rosslynn RPO
Oshawa, ON, Canada, L1J 8L6

http://www.mmpubs.com/

All rights reserved. No part of this book may be reproduced or transmitted in any form or by any means, electronic or mechanical, including photocopying, recording or by any information storage and retrieval system, without written permission from the publisher, except for the inclusion of brief quotations in a review.

Copyright © 2012 by Multi-Media Publications Inc.

Paperback   ISBN-13: 978-1-55489-120-7
Adobe PDF ebook   ISBN-13: 978-1-55489-121-4

Published in Canada. Printed simultaneously in Canada, the United States of America, Australia, and the United Kingdom.

CIP data available from the publisher.

Table of Contents

Preface

What the *Titanic* Story Gives Us

The story of *Titanic* has captivated people for the past 100 years. It stirs our curiosity and emotions, and it is still amazing to think that what was then the largest ship in the world and believed to be unsinkable could face such a disastrous ending. So, how did it all go so wrong? What can be learned from this tragedy? This historic event offers us a rich tapestry of examples about people interactions, power dynamics, communication, leadership, and team working.

On any project, however well you follow the process, there will be people problems to deal with, such as conflict among the team and difficult or overbearing stakeholders to manage. In today's fast changing and chaotic environment, stress is commonplace and emotions can run high. For project managers and leaders, the skills to deal effectively with behavioral issues are more critical than ever before. You need to be just as comfortable managing conflict and motivating your team as you are with planning your work and conducting a risk analysis.

Titanic has given us a valuable legacy. From its fate, we learn what can happen when we overlook the impact of powerful personalities, underlying perceptions, a lack of clear communication, and tensions among the teams.

We will focus on the people aspects of the *Titanic* story, looking at the key stakeholders, their drivers, and their impact on the outcome. What were the leadership problems that ultimately led to the sinking of *Titanic*?

This book is not intended to be a historical reference for all the facts and data about *Titanic*; there is much material published about this on the Internet and in other books. The aim is rather to explore the many people problems that contributed to this disaster, so we can identify useful lessons and reflect on how we can apply these ourselves. Many models and useful techniques have been included:

Behavioral topics covered:
- Balancing power and authority

- Barriers to communication

- Influencing perceptions

- Managing the stages of team development

- Recognizing different kinds of biased thinking such as "group think" and the bandwagon effect

- Recognizing stakeholder dynamics and types of power

- Resolving problems and effective decision making
- Setting up and leading effective teams
- Understanding the causes of conflict and managing conflict.

Why I wrote this book

I wanted to write this book to focus on the key people problems that arise when dealing with projects. In my experience, when faced with challenging deadlines and the pressures that go with managing projects, it's easy to be caught up with ensuring that tasks are completed and checklists are ticked. This will most likely be at the expense of having those difficult conversations with upset stakeholders and disgruntled customers, the people who ultimately determine whether the project is a success or failure.

Typically, project management development focuses on understanding frameworks and methods to help organize work. Project managers certainly need to understand how to plan and control, which makes their life easier, but it just isn't enough. A project's outcome depends entirely on how the people in the project perform and interact. So, project managers also need leadership skills and know-how to get the best from those around them, but they don't tell you this when you first start as a project manager. Even if you were told, it probably did not register until you found yourself having to deal with the complexities people can bring to situations.

There are many books and development courses on the technical aspects of project management, but they don't cover how to deal with people. Plenty on general management and leadership cover the people aspects, but these are too generic and don't relate well to the complexities of working in a project and program context. I found this along my development journey. For about ten years, I seemed to travel along parallel paths; one was in project management, and the other was what I began to think of as personal development, which covered leadership skills. I enjoyed being part of these two worlds, but I could not understand why they were separate.

So, I had been thinking for quite awhile about how to bring these two worlds together and writing about this, but something was still missing. The nature of the subject seemed such that it might be easy to read and follow the words, but not necessarily "feel" it in our gut and "get it." I had been wondering how best to address that.

Last year, I was introduced to Mark Kozak-Holland and his Lessons from History series. The idea of learning from historic events by using them as case studies grabbed me, and I was particularly attracted to the *Titanic* story. On researching this further and learning what went on during the construction of *Titanic* and its maiden voyage, it was very apparent that the problems weren't just technical errors, but very much "a people thing." The missing piece was finally in place, and I could write the book.

I certainly hope you will enjoy reading it and that you get useful insights that will make a difference to the work you do. After a first read, you can dip in and out of different topics as needed to match your priorities. Although the book uses *Titanic's* history, it is important to keep focused on how this is relevant to us today. So, the end of each chapter includes points to consider for your projects. We can use the lessons from the past to warn and prepare us for the future, so we can become more effective project leaders.

By developing your skills, you will gain more choice and flexibility in dealing with situations. The only way to learn how well each technique works for you is to try things—my invitation to you is to "give it a go."

—Ranjit Sidhu

Acknowledgments

I have many people to thank who have supported me and helped shape my thinking in getting me to this point. I am especially grateful to Pamela Ashby for introducing me to Mark Kozak-Holland and for the idea of using the Lessons from History series in the first place. Pamela has painstakingly gone through many revisions of each chapter and continued to offer invaluable support in pulling this book together.

I am very grateful to Mark Kozak-Holland for his enthusiastic support for this book and for sharing so generously his knowledge of Titanic and his experience in writing the books in this series. Thanks also to Mark Baker for translating my thoughts into the visual illustrations you see in the book.

I want to thank my family for their encouragement and support; they help keep me grounded. And a very special mention to my husband who has been on this journey with me every step of the way—thank you for your support and your unwavering belief in me.

Introduction

I t is easy to assume that, in the early 1900s, they worked in a far simpler, stabler world with less complexity and none of the challenges we face today. The turn of the twentieth century was a time of great change, with a technological revolution bringing important developments in engineering and the pioneering use of telegraphs and radio. There were huge opportunities for entrepreneurs with the imagination and energy to take advantage of this new potential.

The White Star Line, the company that owned Titanic, operated in this world. White Star, at the time, struggled to stay profitable. It was an established company, but shipping was a highly competitive business. Their aging fleet of ships was not well placed to benefit from the emerging first-class tourist market or the increase in migrants leaving Europe to resettle in America. The British government had provided funds to White Star's main rival, the Cunard Line, to build two superliners, which meant that their main competitor had faster ships, and White Star could not now afford to fall behind. The pressure was on.

In this context, White Star decided to build three superliners, ships that would be larger and more luxurious than anything the world had seen. They planned to use the latest and most innovative technologies available to provide the ultimate luxury passenger experience.

Outwardly, the building of Titanic seems a straightforward construction project, but in reality, it was about much more than just the mechanics of building a large ship. White Star would bring together new technologies in a way that had never been done. They also aimed to achieve the most luxurious customer experience, but how do you measure luxury? It is very subjective and prone to misinterpretation. They would need to maintain a delicate balance between meeting the technical goals and delivering luxury for their passengers.

As we will see, some very powerful stakeholders were involved. Complex people dynamics, differing viewpoints, and varying priorities created many challenges and potential for conflict along the way. For the maiden voyage, White Star had just a few days to bring together a crew of several hundred people. Establishing temporary teams and getting them to work effectively in such a short time requires clear direction and communication.

The Cunard liners used the latest steam turbine technology, and they were well positioned to lead the field in speed, so White Star decided to highlight luxury with more focus on the experience of the voyage rather than the speed and how quickly they arrived. The marketing strategy was sound in that they had identified a unique benefit that outstripped the value of technology alone.

In this way, a clear vision was established, a good start for any endeavor and one that no doubt helped them gain the financier J. P. Morgan's full support and funding. With such a sound idea and commercial backing from one of the leading transport tycoons of the day, the project surely could not fail...

Business vision   **Financial backing**

... the story begins

CHAPTER 1

Stakeholders and strategy

"Even emperors can't do it all by themselves."
—Bertolt Brecht

W hat drives a project might not be easy to understand at first. It's helpful to stand back, look at the big picture, and think about things such as:

- Is it necessary?

- What will it give us that we don't have already?

- Is this the best way for us to get there?

Taking the time up front to consider these things carefully helps build a secure foundation for the project, ensures the problems are addressed, and helps to make the most of the opportunities available.

17

Understanding the bigger picture also gives us a better appreciation of who the different stakeholders are, what really matters to them, and how best to manage them. If we are aware of the people problems, as well as the process problems, so much more can be learned. As a project's foundations are established, patterns of behavior and influences that might not be either intended or desirable often become the norm. By paying attention to these dynamics early, we can avoid problems later.

Understanding the Strategic Drivers

White Star developed a strategy to invest in emerging technologies and build superliners that offered the highest levels of luxury; something no one else did. At the time, White Star faced many pressures:

- **Strategic pressures**—White Star faced the threat of losing market share. Their current fleet of liners was aging, and they faced a downturn in business.

- **Competitive pressures**—Their main rival Cunard was planning to build the fastest liners with government funding. They were set to become the leaders in the industry for speed.

- **Consumer pressures**—There was a rapid growth in tourist passengers at that time, with new requirements and changing tastes emerging.

- **Environmental pressures**—Many new technologies were becoming available that would change the way ships were built and what they could offer. More migrants were also leaving from Europe to resettle in America.

There were many potential opportunities for White Star to consider.

Strategic pressures
- What is our business?
- Profitability, market share, growth

Environment pressures
- Current trends in market place
- Political, economic, sociological, technical, legal, environment

White Star strategy

Competitive pressures
- Our competitive edge
- Existing opportunities/threats
- Who leads the way?

Consumer pressures
- Changing customer demands
- Emerging new customers
- What are their needs?

Deciding the Strategy

It is interesting to look at how this strategy was decided. This was not the realm of reports and analyses; this strategy was born from relationships. White Star had a longstanding relationship with the shipbuilders Harland and Wolff, a company known as the premier shipbuilders of the world with a reputation for both quality and innovation.

At this time, Bruce Ismay was chairman of White Star, which went back to when his father had been a friend of Harland and Wolff's chairman

Lord Pirrie. The relationship was so close that Lord Pirrie was on the board of White Star as a trusted advisor, which created an unchallenging and very comfortable business relationship between the two companies. Harland and Wolff knew that they would be the chosen supplier for building all White Star's ships, with the only condition being they would not build for White Star's competitors.

Given this climate, it is not surprising that the 1907 strategy meeting that decided the future direction of White Star took place while Ismay and Lord Pirrie dined together at Pirrie's London home. These two men were the only ones involved as they discussed the problems that White Star faced and the options available in the light of stiff competition. Lord Pirrie knew that recent technological developments meant bigger ships could be built, ships much larger than anything yet available. In Ismay's mind, the opportunity for almost unlimited space translated to the notion of luxury, which led to White Star's strategy to sail luxurious superliners.

Figure 1. Lord Pirrie and Bruce Ismay.

Identifying and Understanding the Key Stakeholders

Stakeholders are people who can either help or hinder the project. They might have a role to play, or they might be interested in how things turn out because it affects them directly. Stepping in the stakeholder's shoes to think about "What is in it for me?" from their perspective helps us understand what really motivates our stakeholders and what they need. The underlying motivations are not always spelled out, but paying attention to them offers a real advantage for anyone involved in managing projects and change.

Bruce Ismay

No focus groups and no product development brainstorming sessions were involved in setting the strategy to ensure White Star's commercial future. Bruce Ismay was both a creative entrepreneur and a businessman, and he alone generated the strategy to ensure White Star market leadership and profitability.

Ismay was chairman of White Star and had been made president of the parent conglomerate IMM by J. P. Morgan. By the time this story starts, he was used to being in control, and he enjoyed a very powerful and influential position. His father had been chairman of White Star before him, and this must have affected his approach to the challenges his role presented. Perhaps he wanted to make his mark and differentiate himself from what his father had achieved. Knowing what is important to stakeholders and what they value are important aspects of management.

A leading businessman, Ismay mingled freely in high society and enjoyed a very privileged lifestyle. As the world changed, and White Star became less competitive in the face of greater competition, he would have realized that his lifestyle, as well as the company, was at risk and tried to protect them. In making the first-class passenger experience his priority, he was choosing a benefit he could relate to so he could target customers he knew well. He was well placed to lead worldwide publicity for the new shipbuilding project.

J. P. Morgan

Widely recognized as the richest man in the world at that time, J. P. Morgan was clearly a very influential and powerful figure. This man came to epitomize security, with everything about him exuding stability and confidence. Although Ismay moved in high circles, Morgan's society was higher still—he was later invited to the coronation of King George V. He clearly had much faith in Ismay, having made him president of his huge IMM conglomerate.

Morgan was a key player in the U.S. financial markets and helped restore order after the 1907 Bankers' Panic when the New York Stock Exchange fell almost 50% from its peak the previous year, and there were many runs on the banks. The crisis could have deepened, but Morgan pledged large sums of his money and convinced other New York bankers to do the same to shore up the banking system.

Morgan financed the White Star shipbuilding project through a major share issue, giving it his stamp of approval and ensuring it became viewed with the surety that was so much a trademark of his life and endeavors.

Lord Pirrie

Lord Pirrie's obituary in a 1924 issue of the Times describes him as "a man of vision" and "one of the world's greatest business men." Pirrie had joined Harland and Wolff as an apprentice when he was fifteen, and it took him just twelve years to become a partner in the organization. This man was not only a technologist and at the forefront of groundbreaking developments in shipbuilding techniques, but was also known to be a shrewd businessman who knew how to grasp opportunities. The Times recounts how "on one occasion, a well-known shipping company asked, towards the end of a week, for tenders for the construction of a new liner from a number of leading shipbuilding companies. On the Monday morning, there were written replies from all the shipbuilding companies with the exception of Harland and Wolff. When the letters were received, Lord Pirrie was closeted with the head of the company and secured the contract. He never allowed the grass to grow below his feet."

Perhaps it is no surprise then that Lord Pirrie and Bruce Ismay were good friends and closely linked through their business relationships. With Pirrie on the board of White Star, the two men would have been certain of one another's support. They were powerful, successful, very confident, and interested in the potential of emerging technologies. The financial backing of Morgan gave the project full validation, and having the involvement of powerful

and influential figures such as Ismay and Lord
Pirrie meant it had more kudos than probably any
other project of its day.

Bruce Ismay
- Luxurious ships like no other
- A great passenger experience and an increased revenue flow

Lord Pirrie
- Ships using the latest technological advance

J. P. Morgan
- Money making venture leading to good return on investment

Agreeing the Way Forward

White Star Chairman Ismay had identified a
gap in the marketplace and had confirmed that
it was technologically possible to meet this need
competitively. Full funding had been achieved, and
it was "all systems go."

Things looked promising; they had a clear goal
and a sensible approach. White Star would invest
in new technologies and build three superliners
offering the most luxurious experience available—
ships that could offer good service for more than
twenty years. The plan was to deliver two ships,

each in four years, and then follow with the third using the funds generated by the first two. The three men saw this as a great opportunity, and they were clearly very confident, as they were prepared to build the first two ships almost in parallel. The organizational relationships core to the project were well established and endorsed by friendships and common values. The supply chain was established because of the longstanding relationship with Harland and Wolff. The business case was clear about targeting luxury over speed, and they planned to achieve at least 75% of the revenue from the first-class passengers.

Their reputations reflected a seemingly perfect blend of innovation and sound business sense. They were confident they could be innovative, take risks, and be successful as a result. Nor was money a concern, as the richest man in the world had offered to fund the project.

Doing a Sanity Check

It's easy to think that all this happened "way back when," when the world was a simpler place and projects were straightforward. However, let's not forget, this was a time of fast-paced change, and huge technological breakthroughs were made. It was an entrepreneurial era, with a growing tourist industry for the upper classes and mass migration. Although there had been global financial panic, it was still an optimistic time, reflecting the turn of a new century and all the new possibilities that would bring.

Ismay and Lord Pirrie were planning to ride this wave. They would bring together the latest technologies and materials in a new way to create their luxurious superliners.

It was a huge undertaking, both in sheer scale and because of the complexity caused by integrating so many new technologies in a way that had never been done. This project would be a huge investment, so before going any further, a "sanity check" should be carried out, which asks simple questions such as:

- What are the possibilities?

- Is this feasible and doable? Will this address the underlying problems?

- What could go wrong, and how can we prepare for that?

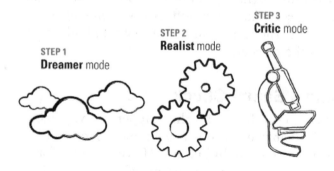

STEP 1
Dreamer mode

STEP 2
Realist mode

STEP 3
Critic mode

A useful model for doing this is the Disney Creativity Strategy from the Walt Disney Company, modeled by Robert Dilts. This model suggests looking at ideas and plans from three perspectives: first, from an innovative, creative perspective to find the ideas. Then, these ideas should go through a reality check—is it doable and how? The third step is to become the critic to test the idea for robustness and risks to think about all the downsides.

Step 1—Dreamer *mode*

In this space, people are encouraged to imagine new ideas and options. Ismay was clearly creative in devising the idea of the luxury experience; no one else had imagined that yet.

Step 2—Realist *mode*

This is when the ideas are turned into a plan. How will we approach this? What is realistically possible? This step provides the opportunity to investigate logistics, time, money aspects, and make trade-offs where they are needed.

Step 3—Critic *mode*

Now, play devil's advocate and intentionally look at the project from the perspective of what could go wrong.

Where are the flaws? Will the customers appreciate this? Is there anything here that might be redundant or unnecessary? What about from a technical or legal perspective—have all the safety and regulatory angles been covered?

This method works best where different people step into the roles completely, even to the extent of moving to different rooms when exploring these different positions. Stakeholders, team members, and customers can all take part to ensure a fully balanced approach.

In the case of the Titanic project, Ismay seemed the only representative presenting the requirements of the first-class passengers. There is little evidence of research or customer involvement to check how important some of these might have been.

Other directors from White Star don't seem to have been consulted, nor were other expert opinions sought to test ideas. Although our main players thought they were on sound ground and that their innovations and plans were well thought out, they likely had a narrow view of the criteria that could make this venture successful.

Ismay's lifestyle in high society meant he knew what customers wanted, but this made it difficult for him to step back and look at things objectively as a leader of White Star. This becomes important later when decisions were made that prioritized luxury over safety in the specification—but based on what?

Ensuring a Strong Start

At the beginning of a new venture, it's easy to be excited and carried away with the possibilities. Often, the people involved in generating new ideas are then unable to take a critical viewpoint, to think about the possible downsides and whether the approach is robust and sufficiently sound. Stopping to do a sanity check before jumping in with both feet helps overcome this.

Key points to consider for your projects:

- Who are the key players involved?

- What is important to them, and what are their expectations?

- Who are your customers?

- Are their requirements clearly understood and well represented?

- What are the possible downsides of following the agreed approach?

- Think about what could go wrong and what would help you and your team challenge the chosen approach.

CHAPTER 2

Definitions and Design

"The certainties of one age are the problems of the next."
—R. H. Tawney

The goal was established and funding approved, so now they could start work on designing and building the biggest and most luxurious ships in the world.

With any project, many common mistakes that stem from mistaken assumptions are made in the early stages

- By senior managers that what is obvious to them must be obvious to the rest of the team. For example, luxury means very different things to different people.

- That the senior manager's definition of the problem and solution should be accepted because they have given much thought to it or have more experience. Even though the overall goal was very clear, the real complexity of what was asked had not been thought through and was unfolding throughout the design phase.

- That decisions made by senior managers and the normal ways of working cannot be questioned. The imposed time scales were very tight, but fortunately, the teams were already used to working together.

Defining what Luxury Means

The project mantra of luxury over speed was clear from the start. Everyone involved understood that they did not aim to cross the Atlantic in record time—but did they have a clear idea of what they all meant by *luxury*? It seems common sense that a millionaire will define luxury differently from someone working for a minimum wage. Speed can easily be measured, but how do you measure a concept such as luxury? How would they know when it was luxurious enough?

Ismay had very particular ideas in his head about what he meant by luxury and other elements of the customer experience, but the design team might have had difficulty envisioning them because they related to these concepts differently. They were probably more used to working with physical, tangible things and interpreted luxury as "best," opting to go with the highest level of safety and incorporate all the latest and advanced safety technologies.

Interpreting Through Our Filters

We each interpret the world around us differently.
Our understanding and perceptions are shaped by
the way we process information, which is unique to
each of us because we can only take in very limited
detail through our senses in any moment, yet we
continuously try to absorb a range of information
from our surroundings.

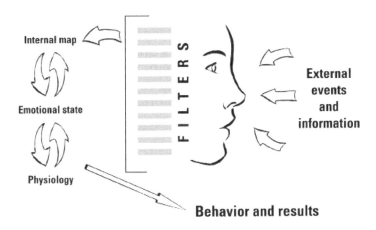

To avoid being overwhelmed by all this, we
filter it and make an internal map that is our
representation of the incoming information. The way
these filters work is unique to each person, as they
are based on experiences, memories, values, beliefs,
assumptions held, and our cultural environment.

Filters delete, distort, and generalize information
as it comes in:

- Deletion occurs when we focus only on some
  parts of the information and overlook the
  rest.

- Distortion implies we misrepresent the available information, so we might exaggerate the importance of something or underestimate it completely.

- Generalization leads us to draw universal conclusions about how things are from just a few examples.

So, we each end up with our version of what's going on, which in turn affects our emotions and behaviors. Our brains sensibly take a mental shortcut to process the information efficiently. It's a bit like creating a map; we can't include every aspect and detail on a map, yet the overall image is invaluable in helping us find our way around and decide the best route to take.

Being able to filter information helps us with problem solving, making decisions, learning, and discovery. This shortcut processing helps us when we face complex problems and incomplete information, enabling us to find solutions where more extensive searching and analyzing might not be desirable. Daily examples include when we use a rule of thumb or an educated guess.

Although the team had specifications for features such as the three-story staircase and the swimming pool, which contributed to the luxury experience, they very likely made educated guesses about what the luxurious experience really meant.

Understanding the Complexities Involved

Ismay's core project goal of luxury, rather than speed, was kept in mind at every stage, and each innovation was considered from this perspective. For this reason, a U-shaped hull design was selected against the traditional V shape, which would have created a faster ship, but one that would have had less room for the spacious accommodations and facilities Ismay wanted. The liner design would create the largest moving vehicle ever built—the technological challenges of meeting Ismay's design expectations were enormous.

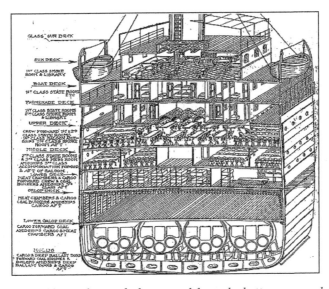

Figure 2. Shows the ten decks, named from the bottom upward: Lower orlop, orlop, lower, middle, upper, saloon shelter, bridge, promenade, and ship deck, named alphabetically A, B, C, D, E, F, and G. The passenger decks were the promenade deck, bridge deck, shelter deck, saloon deck, tipper deck, middle deck, and lower deck.

The design specification included the creation of a spectacular first-class entrance stairway that cut right through three decks. There were to be three elevators at the forward first-class main entrance, and each was to have capacity for ten passengers. There was also to be a heated swimming pool and Turkish baths. The marketing concept was to raise the standard of everything about the passengers' earlier experiences; third class equated with second class on other shipping lines, second equated with first, leaving White Star's first class "in a class of its own" and more luxurious than any other cruising experience of its time. All the planned features were very impressive, but making the vision a reality presented serious challenges for the architects.

Working to Tight Deadlines

The project schedule was that the design for the first two ships (*Olympic* and *Titanic*) would be generated between April 1907 and July 1908. Then, the White Star directors would approve the final designs, and an agreement would be signed to start construction. This was a major task to complete within a relatively short time.

The design process was iterative and subdivided into several phases, during which the design was developed in increasing degrees of detail. The project reflected many principles of today's Agile development techniques, as they didn't have the time to plan every detail from the start and allowed the detailed requirements to evolve as they progressed. They also used what-if scenarios to assess risks and test assumptions, using a fifteen-foot long shipbuilder's model.

The design process had to translate Ismay's requirements into the drawings, specifications, and other technical data needed to build the liners. The naval architects led the process, working with marine and production engineers and structural designers. Teams of design draftsmen and estimators would also have been involved, creating a project structure of some complexity.

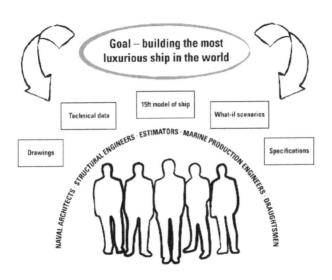

Aligning the Team and Working Practices

It would be easy to create an image of the poor old architects wanting to stick to functional aspects and feeling frustrated that Ismay pushed them down the line of luxury for its own sake; but there is no evidence of this. At this stage, he had communicated a clear direction, and everyone worked hard toward it. The architects bought into the goal so completely that aesthetics became a dominant aspect of the design. It is said that Ismay himself asked how many engines the ship had because the design showed four funnels. It turns out that the fourth funnel was just a dummy, introduced by the architects to make the ship seem as powerful as its main competitors were. The architects knew that even if it were an illusory effect, *Olympic* and *Titanic* would need to look bigger and better than any other ship.

Harland and Wolff was a leading organization of its time, and the naval architects and draftsmen employed on the Titanic design would have included some of the very best professionals in their fields.

Figure 3. The spacious drawing office at Harland and Wolff in Belfast.

They had a clear goal, and each understood the part they played in achieving that goal, giving them a strong sense of purpose, which was the glue that held them together. The project team was well structured with well-defined roles based on each person's area of expertise. They also had clear reporting lines with established hierarchies and processes to follow, enabling them to get on with the job.

In such an innovative environment, there is more uncertainty and a need for creativity. Fortunately, the relationship between White Star and Harland and Wolff meant that the teams were already well established, which would have helped with more open communication and flexibility. Had this not been the case, the standard working practices and hierarchies expected might well have been too rigid and hindered innovation.

Checking for Common Understanding

Designing and building the *Olympic*-class ships involved taking a giant step forward and working on a different scale of complexity. In many respects, the project ran like clockwork, carried through by having a well-established team and a clear goal.

What was missing was an understanding of how to measure luxury and know when it had been achieved. This goal came only from Ismay, and no one else was involved in defining what *luxury* meant.

Key points to consider for your projects:

- Is what is obvious to me just as obvious to others?

- Do I, and does my team, fully understand what is required and what it will look like?

- How will you know whether what you deliver will be acceptable?

- Are team members sharing ideas and talking to one another to check their understanding?

- Is the team comfortable about challenging ideas and decisions?

- Talk about the assumptions held and test them.

CHAPTER 3

Construction and Compromise

*"Things which matter most must never be at
the mercy of things which matter least."*
—Goethe

I nevitably, during any project, problems and
obstacles will arise. This is normal, and it is not
the fact they occur that is a problem, but it is
how they are managed and resolved that makes a
difference to how successful a project is. Managing
problems effectively means dealing with them
quickly, learning from them, and remembering to
keep an eye out for them in the first place.

It is worth keeping three key points in mind:

- **Resolve problems quickly**—This is
  important for keeping up the momentum
  and pace of working. If it takes too long, it
  can lead to unnecessary delays or just make
  things worse.

41

- **Learn from previous problems**—Make sure the same problems don't keep recurring. This wastes time and energy and demotivates the team. It is important to build in regular reviews and keep applying the lessons learned.

- **Look for signs of potential problems**—By actively looking for early warning signs and dealing with them, you can help the project run much more smoothly. Many problems that occur stem from misunderstandings between people.

Inspecting the Designs

On July 29, 1908, approaching the end of the design phase, Ismay, Lord Pirrie, and a few other White Star directors attended a review meeting. On September 17, the order was given to proceed with the construction. The intervening seven or so weeks must have been a very fraught time for the team. Although the design was approved in principle, several issues were raised, and there must have been a series of later discussions before the approval to go ahead was given.

Ismay's vision for achieving "luxury and space" was very clear in his mind, but he and the design team had a different understanding about how these factors would be balanced with the safety requirements of the ship. Ismay was particularly unhappy about these areas:

- **Number of lifeboat stations**—The design initially included sixteen lifeboat stations, each carrying four lifeboats, making sixty-four. The design had housed the lifeboats on the ship's highest deck, which was also the promenade deck where the first-class passengers could stroll. Ismay believed the panoramic views were a key feature for his first-class customers, so he had problems with quadruple-stacked lifeboats blocking those views. Ismay felt strongly that the lifeboats would ruin *Titanic's* chances of commercial success. The lifeboats would have to be moved!

- **The large dining room**—Ismay wanted the dining room to be the largest room ever to go to sea. He had in mind that it would seat 532 people and host a variety of balls and gala dinners to make the voyage an unforgettable experience. The architects had not achieved this because they had included sealed multiple watertight compartments in the hull of the ship.

  Electric sliding doors could seal areas of the ship in just thirty seconds and reduce the likelihood of flooding if a collision occurs. For Ismay's vision to be realized, three of the bulkhead walls would have to be shortened so they did not cut through the dining room, but then they wouldn't reach the top deck and would be just ten feet above the waterline!

- **The double hull for extra safety**—The design included a double hull along the bottom of the ship, continuing up the sides and providing an all-around double skin. This offered enormous safety benefit but at the cost of what Ismay regarded as a huge reduction in space. A double hull would take away fifteen feet from a ninety-two-foot beam—another constraint to Ismay's vision of ultimate space and luxury. The compromise limited the double hull just to the bottom, seven feet deep, and well below the waterline.

Balancing the Requirements

This was a difficult situation. Ismay wanted fundamental changes made to the design the architects had recommended—changes that would affect the vessel's safety. How were they to proceed?

Resolving Problems

The architects were pushed to compromise, and Ismay was quick to dictate solutions based on his interpretation of the value of space and luxury for the customer. He stepped straight into solution mode, but perhaps he should have stepped back to explore multiple perspectives on the problems he perceived, rather than just his own.

When an obstacle on a project has been identified, it helps to explore it fully to define precisely what the problem is. Time spent doing this is well worth it, because the way the problem is defined influences later steps in decision making. Usually, we're too quick to jump to conclusions and, as *Titanic's* architects discovered, it can be just too tempting to give in to pressure and just take one person's word for it. For a more robust resolution of problems, try this simple process:

- **Clearly articulate the problem**—If a problem is well defined, it lends itself to different possible solutions, which can then be assessed and considered. In the case of Titanic, was the obscuring of the ocean views really a problem to first-class passengers—in what way? If a balanced sample of potential passengers had been asked, they might not have found it a problem at all. We won't ever know, but they might even have found the sight of lifeboats reassuring.

- **Expose and challenge assumptions—** Every problem, however simple it might seem, comes with a long list of assumptions attached. The trouble is that many of these assumptions might be inaccurate or misguided because of the filtering that occurs when we take in information and form our internal maps. By surfacing these assumptions and testing or validating them, we help fill in, or "undistort," the filtering that has occurred.

  Ismay assumed the large dining area space would help make the voyage unforgettable. What were his grounds for believing this? Was it perhaps based on his experience? Testing this assumption could have highlighted that the space itself didn't matter, but what was done in that space would make the voyage unforgettable.

  Testing assumptions effectively needs people to play devil's advocate to help surface the underlying thoughts and the constraints applied. To achieve this, time needs to be made available, and an open and safe culture should be encouraged, so the team feels comfortable challenging and questioning one another.

- **Chunk up**—To get a different perspective, look at the bigger picture and explore the wider terrain around the problem. Does it still look like the same problem when it is viewed in a much wider context? Were there other places *Titanic's* passengers could walk to see the ocean views? Taking into account all the other ways that passengers would have an "unforgettable voyage," was the reduced dining space area such a big problem?

- **Get specific and break the problem down**—Now, break the problem into smaller parts. Possibly, some parts of the problem may be okay and need no change. Reducing a problem into smaller bite-size chunks can trigger some useful insights and help prioritize those aspects that must be dealt with, making a resolution seem more doable.

- **Identify alternatives**—Now that you have a well-defined problem that has been fully explored, you can understand its scale and look at different solutions. More choices create more flexibility, but always aim for more than two options; otherwise, you just create an either-or dilemma.

- **Consider the consequences for each alternative**—Get others involved in helping you do this, so you can see the alternatives from multiple perspectives and weigh up the pros and cons.

Resolving problems:

1. Clearly articulate the problem

2. Expose and challenge assumptions

3. Chunk up

4. Get specific and break down the problem

5. Identify alternatives

6. Consider consequences of each alternative

Compromising

None of this happened in the case of the Titanic project; the architects felt pressured and design compromises were made purely based on Ismay's perspective. They agreed to:

- Reduce the lifeboats to thirty-two instead of the sixty-four originally planned

- Expand the dining-room space and reduce the height of the bulkheads

- Sacrifice the double hull design completely, leaving just a seven-foot double bottom to the ship

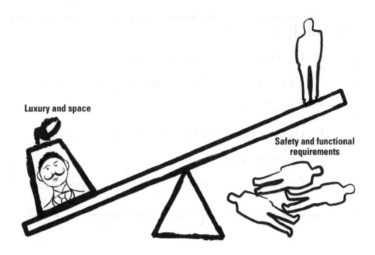

Luxury and space

Safety and functional requirements

Reflecting on Lessons Learned

This would have been a sensible time to step back and reflect on how things were progressing and how things had been done so far, so the lessons could be incorporated into the next stage.

As well as doing this for the work carried out, it can also be done on how the work has been managed and the way the design review was conducted. It is useful to do this from multiple perspectives. For example:

- How did the review go from the customer White Star's perspective?

- How did it go from Harland and Wolff, the architect and shipbuilder's perspective?

- How would the review meeting have looked to an objective observer, such as a "fly on the wall"?

In the design review meeting, between four and five hours were devoted to discussing décor and fittings, but no more than ten minutes were given to lifeboat capacity. This might have seemed right for the White Star party but possibly very frustrating for the architects from Harland and Wolff. An outside observer looking at this objectively would have seen that it was very unbalanced considering the importance of the safety features in the bigger scheme of things.

What was going on here to create an environment where the focus was squarely on décor and fittings rather than safety features? It is very possible that the architects did not mind this at all. Let's face it; there is probably more to say about the grandeur of the three-story staircase or the heated swimming pool and Turkish baths than there is about the width and capacity of the double hull.

It would be natural for the architects and shipbuilders to be excited and overly positive about the Titanic project, as it was such an innovative and high profile undertaking. It would be easy to be carried away and too confident about success. Already, it was said *Titanic's* design made it function like a huge lifeboat, so a general acceptance of this made the compromises seem less risky.

Recognizing Biased Thinking

So far, the architects had accepted Ismay's views and had changed their design to match his specific vision. The perception had been building that the ship was very safe, and the team seems not to have thought that the compromises would endanger the passengers at all. The filtering and mental shortcut processing that occurs in the way people absorb information can lead to this kind of skewed and biased thinking. An anchoring bias occurs.

This is when people over rely on set information to govern their thinking. In this case, from the beginning, the team had been designing the ship to be the best with the very latest safety features. New technologies enabled innovative safety features, the scale of which had never been seen, to be incorporated. All this helped instill huge confidence in the perception that this was an extremely safe, robust ship.

An anchor was set based on this information, and it acted as their default starting point. Using a scale of 1 to 10, with 10 being the safest ship ever, their starting point becomes anchored at 10. From this point, any new information that needs processing is compared with the new starting point. So, instead of having to think from scratch about how safe the ship is, where on the scale it should be positioned, the brain takes a shortcut by going to the anchor because that is now the starting point. Then, a certain amount can be adjusted up or down, depending on the new information.

Once a bias anchor like this is set, it then affects any future decision making. So, when Ismay suggested that the number of lifeboats be reduced and the bulkhead walls shortened, the bias remained that safety was still the highest standard, and the compromises didn't seem serious. Had they considered the compromises one at a time and readjusted that starting anchor position with each compromise, they would have come to appreciate more fully the combined effect of these compromises.

Agreeing on the Way Forward

The team did very well working to the tight schedule
set for the design phase. A major milestone had been
reached with the designs being agreed. The contract
was signed, and the construction phase began with
the first ship Olympic, with the Titanic construction
following. Compromises had been made, though,
and a strong bias in thinking had been established
that affected how problems were resolved. From this
point, Ismay alone assumed responsibility for any
further changes to the specification—this was not an
ideal situation.

Key points to consider for your projects:

- Do the same problems keep recurring? If so, why?

- When problems occur, is sufficient time spent on clarifying and understanding them?

- Are problems explored from multiple perspectives by getting input from different people?

- Consider multiple options for dealing with a problem and weigh the consequences for each option.

- What compromises have been made on your project, and how will these affect what has been promised?

- Think about a variety of what-if scenarios to help you and your team challenge common assumptions and biases.

CHAPTER 4

Marketing and Media

"The eye sees only what the mind is prepared to comprehend."
—Robertson Davies

O nce the main construction phase for *Olympic* ended, the ship was launched into the sea and towed to the wharf for fitting out. Now, the vessel's awe-inspiring proportions were even more visible to the public, and interest mounted in what was possibly the largest project in the world. Ismay was very interested in spreading the right publicity messages, but we begin to see that he was much less interested in communicating with his construction teams and his crews, leaving them to glean information from what was publicly available. Unquestioning optimism might be an appropriate perspective for a passenger, but what happens when the captain and crew feel that way?

Influencing Perceptions

White Star's publicists were no novices when it came to organizing a marketing campaign. A range of interviews given to the media supported a large-scale poster advertising campaign. Apparently, they took more than 150 photographs. There was much interest in the launch. The team's efforts were rewarded, and about a third of the population of Belfast turned up to witness *Olympic* slide into the sea. The ship was the largest manufactured object ever moved, and public interest was at its height.

Figure 4. This IMM advertisement specifically points to one of the most important safety features available—the wireless telegraph for ship-to-ship and ship-to-shore communication.

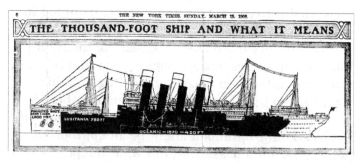

Figure 5. The New York Times *announcement highlighted the scale up in ships from the current line to the competition to the planned. In twelve years, ships had scaled up 400% in size.*

Ismay had *Olympic* painted in light gray and ocher colors especially for the occasion. This was a common practice in those days, as the striking contrast made the ship appear much more clearly in the black-and-white photographs. Immediately after the launch, the hull was repainted.

The event had been very successful and ensured that *Olympic* remained a topic of public interest while Titanic was constructed back in the dry dock. When *Olympic* went through the sea trials, the results were phenomenal. Not only did she gain her seaworthiness certificate, but also she was even faster and even more maneuverable than expected. A pattern of escalating success was building!

Jumping on the Bandwagon

The bandwagon effect occurs when many people start to share a belief or beliefs. As support for an idea builds, the momentum increases, and more and more people start to share the popular way of thinking because others do and without considering their actions. In effect, people begin to behave with a herd instinct rather than remaining independent and thinking for themselves. Marketing and political lobbying techniques rely greatly on the bandwagon effect to achieve ever-increasing support and exponential growth in their following.

Believing Publicity Promises

The project was surrounded by success stories, and the project team might have believed that nothing could go wrong. Although many safety features had been compromised, even before the construction had started, interestingly, the marketing statements communicated remained the same. There was a confidence that the broad hull design, its size, and the advanced safety features and technologies would protect it from any danger.

When *Olympic* became operational, its track record was already far from equal to the expectations set by the publicity promises. She had three major incidents during her first trips across the Atlantic, including a collision with the Royal Navy cruiser HMS *Hawke* in the harbor. A trial followed that pronounced, "The *Olympic* was to blame for the manner in which she came into the path to which the *Hawke* was entitled." *Hawke* was much damaged in the accident.

Setting the Tone

This could have significantly reduced faith in the *Olympic*-class ships, both for the project team and for the public, but interestingly, the positive momentum of success that had built seemed to ensure that the opposite became true. The event was understood to provide further evidence of the sheer strength of these groundbreaking ships. After the sinking of Titanic, an article appeared in the *Washington Times* describing how White Star's Captain Smith had used the *Hawke* incident as an example of the strength of the superliners:

That Captain Smith believed Titanic and the *Olympic*
to be absolutely unsinkable is recalled by a man who
had a conversation with the veteran commander
on a recent voyage of the *Olympic*. The talk was
concerning the accident in which the British warship
Hawke rammed the *Olympic*.

"The commander of the *Hawke* was entirely to
blame," commented a young officer who was in the
group. "He was 'showing off' his warship before a
throng of passengers and made a miscalculation."

Captain Smith smiled enigmatically at the theory
advanced by his subordinate, but made no comment
as to this view of the mishap.

"Anyhow," declared Captain Smith, "the *Olympic*
is unsinkable, and Titanic will be the same when she
is put in commission. "Why," he continued, "either of
these vessels could be cut in halves and each half
would remain afloat indefinitely. The non-sinkable
vessel has been reached in these two wonderful
craft." "I venture to add," concluded Captain Smith,
"that even if the engines and boilers of these vessels
were to fall through their bottoms the vessels would
remain afloat."

Captain Smith would be in command of Titanic
on its maiden voyage, and the depth of his confidence
is important in setting the scene for what follows.
Take away the power of the bandwagon effect and
the effectiveness of the publicity accompanying
Olympic's launch, and the interpretation of the
Hawke incident could have been very different. The
same incident could have highlighted safety issues
associated with such large vessels, but a pattern had
been set.

Now, everything seemed to endorse the view—
the *Olympic*-class ships were unsinkable. Captain

Smith had a reputation for being in command of White Star's newest ships on their maiden voyages, and he had become known as "the Millionaires' Captain." He was enthusiastic about innovations in shipbuilding and sailing across the Atlantic in Adriatic, some years before the *Olympic*-class vessels, he had declared, "I cannot imagine any condition which would cause a ship to flounder... Modern shipping has gone beyond that."

Reinforcing Perceptions

Ismay realized that the perception that these ships were nearly unsinkable was invaluable as part of White Star's marketing campaign. The White Star Line publicity booklet of May 1911 published: "Today, ships are amongst the greatest civilizing agencies of the age, and the White Star liners *Olympic* and Titanic—eloquent testimonies to the progress of mankind, as shown in the conquest of mind over matter—will rank high in the achievements of the 20th century." This type of communication further reinforced the claims of invincibility of the *Olympic*-class ships.

In 1911, the engineering magazine Shipbuilder interviewed the project architects who described the principal features of the ship, including the emerging technologies used for safety. The magazine later published an article that described the construction project and concluded the ships were nearly unsinkable. The article received little attention, but on June 1, 1911, this all changed when the *Irish News* and *Belfast Morning News* contained a report on the launching of Titanic. The article included a description of the system of watertight compartments and electric watertight doors and repeated the assertion that Titanic was nearly unsinkable.

Ismay's excellent publicity campaign set up a sequence of events that kept building the public perception the *Olympic*-class ships were unsinkable. The bandwagon effect was in full flow...

 Key points to consider for your projects:

- Can I identify the groups with whom I need to communicate?

- Do my communications need to influence their perceptions? If so, how?

- What do I communicate, and how often?

- What expectations have been set with people around me?

- Can I follow through on any promises I make?

CHAPTER 5

Changes and Consequences

"Change is certain. Progress is not."
—E. H. Carr

As work progresses, it is quite normal for there to be changes to what was agreed and planned, which might be because the work was not defined clearly enough at the beginning. But even if that was done very well, outside circumstances might have changed, or people might change their minds about what they want or how they would like it.

The way these changes are managed can have a big impact on a project's outcome. Having a change control process in place helps you assess and understand a change's impact before a decision is made to go ahead with it—the process side of it. However, the people side of it will affect how well this works. Having the right people involved in a process ensures a balanced view for making objective decisions about a project. This was not so with Titanic—this culture did not encourage involvement in decisions that came from the top.

Recording the Changes

As work progressed with *Titanic*, they faced many changes:

- **Reducing the number of lifeboats—** During the first design review, Harland and Wolff had agreed to reduce the number of lifeboats to thirty-two from the sixty-four Carlisle's plan originally recommended. Ismay later wanted to reduce the lifeboats still further to sixteen, to provide more space for verandas, sundecks, and sports by having just one lifeboat hanging from each davit. Carlisle had opted for an innovative design that enabled four wooden lifeboats to hang from each davit. Ismay now asked for this to be changed, which undermined Carlisle's contribution. The sixteen lifeboats now planned were the minimum required by the regulations, so four collapsible lifeboats were added, making the lifeboat capacity 25% above regulation standards.

- **Additional facilities for first-class passengers—**After returning from *Olympic's* maiden voyage, Ismay requested further changes be made to Titanic. He wanted to convert one promenade to create extra first-class staterooms and suites, two of these with private verandas. This would provide additional revenue per voyage. He also wanted to create a trellised café overlooking the sea. His focus was on maximizing the first-class passenger's experience and increasing profits, and he wasn't stepping back to look at the wider picture.

- **Reducing amount of ship vibration—** During the trials and the Olymics's maiden voyage, a troubling amount of vibration had been noted. To correct this, reinforced steel was added in key areas, including where the double bottom met the main hull—a difficult change considered important for the ship's performance.

Assessing the Knock-on Effect of Changes

The impact of these changes should have been assessed thoroughly—not just the impact to safety, but also the knock-on effect in time, cost, and benefits, and an assessment of the risks that might have been introduced. There would be more revenue from having additional first-class suites, but this should have been balanced against the increase in risk caused by reducing the number of lifeboats. The benefit of creating a trellised café should again have been balanced against the extra cost and time it took to build. Viewpoints from different experts would have helped the team understand the consequences fully, especially those of reducing the lifeboats.

Identifying Alternate Options

Other ways for providing what was requested should
also have been considered. Ismay didn't care about
the exact number of lifeboats; what he was trying
to achieve was ultimate luxury for his first-class
passengers. So, other ways of stacking the lifeboats
or storing them could have been explored. Chunking
up to look at the bigger picture can help with
thinking about alternatives.

Deciding Whether to Accept the Changes

Only after this assessment is done can a
recommendation be made to help in deciding
whether to accept a change. However, Ismay's
requests were treated almost like orders. Without
further challenge, the additional changes were
decided by a single voice.

A simple change control process:

1. Record the changes

2. Assess the knock-on effect

3. Identify and evaluate alternate options

4. Decide whether to accept the change

Questioning the Decision

Carlisle resisted this further reduction in the
number of lifeboats but shortly afterward left the
company. He had started work at Harland and Wolff
as an apprentice at sixteen and had worked there
for forty years! The resignation was unexpected, as

it was the popular belief that Carlisle in time would take over Lord Pirrie's role in the organization.

Carlisle had been the shipyard's general manager and chief draftsman when the *Olympic* and Titanic were ordered, and he was responsible for coordinating the designs. He played a central role in the design and equipment of the *Olympic*-class ships, and he was a core member of the team. Although Lord Pirrie had almost entirely designed the *Olympic* and Titanic construction, Carlisle had contributed the details, the decorations, the equipment, and the general arrangements including the innovative lifeboat davit design. Carlisle was Lord Pirrie's brother-in-law, and he had stated that he found working with him difficult.

Recognizing Different Types of Power

Carlisle did not have the power to affect the lifeboat decision. As general manager, he obviously had a senior position, but clearly, the power wielded by Ismay was stronger and impossible to resist. When making decisions, sources of power are a key contributing factor. Power can come from a range of sources that vary in their impact:

- **Reward power**—This stems from the person being able to offer rewards—money, recognition, security, offering status. Ismay and Lord Pirrie were each in positions where they could do this.

- **Coercive power**—This is a fear-based source of power, where a manager or leader makes it clear that if team members do not comply, there will be negative repercussions.

65

Whether Ismay attempted to coerce Carlisle is unclear, but his leaving so suddenly certainly seems to imply it. His successor and other team members would have been concerned about questioning decisions, as doing so had clearly been disastrous for Carlisle.

- **Legitimate power**—This sort of power comes because of the formal position of a manager or leader. They have legitimate authority to give orders and expect people to follow. Carlisle was the shipyard's general manager and had much legitimate power. Lord Pirrie and Ismay also had legitimate power, but theirs was strengthened by being combined with reward power, some expert power, and maybe even coercive power.

- **Expert power**—This power is based on knowledge and expertise in a particular area. Most stakeholders for this project could show technical competence and a specialized skill, but sometimes, this was not enough to influence those holding reward and coercive power.

Changing Team Dynamics

When Carlisle left, Thomas Andrews became the general manager and took over this leading role in the project. He had been involved in the design of the *Olympic*-class ships from the beginning and had reported to Carlisle. So, the team members would have had to get used to his change of role, but they wouldn't have needed to know him as a person from scratch. Although he increased his legitimate power through the promotion, his team probably did not see it that way, as they had known him a long time in a position at a lower level.

Being newly promoted, he unlikely would have challenged Ismay and Lord Pirrie, and the way Carlisle left would have discouraged him too. There was a common goal to work toward, and the team would have refocused quickly, given the extremely tight deadlines ahead.

Avoiding Challenge and Conforming to the Norm

There seems a clear hierarchical structure, with top-down "command and control" type leadership. This environment typically has a very directive style of leadership. The people at the top are expected to set the direction and have the answers, with those below following their orders. In this culture, there tends to be little challenging of decisions, and there might be a fear of doing so.

Ismay and Lord Pirrie were both strong characters and strong leaders. The group tendency would subconsciously have been to follow their example, even if those views contradicted their own. Combine this with the backdrop of overconfidence in the ships' safety. Remember this perception had been building over a long time, and the hugely successful publicity campaign had made it stronger. The view was that the ship was a lifeboat in itself, and the only need for lifeboats would be to save passengers from other ships in distress.

The team absorbed the opinion of their leaders about the ship's safety, so they were more likely to accept any compromises made without assessing these critically. In this sort of culture, people try to fit in and conform, and they can jump quickly at decisions without looking at different options. This makes it very difficult for people to have opposing opinions, as this places them outside the main group. Remaining as a member of the group means a person will not be blamed for a faulty decision, as the whole group makes all decisions.

In the Harland and Wolff community, this type of conformity would have been compelling. It was a tight community, with staff typically joining the workforce at sixteen and remaining until retirement.

Negative outcomes of conformity:

- Examining few alternatives

- Not being critical of each other's ideas

- Not seeking objective expert opinion

- Being highly selective in gathering information

Confirming Preconceptions

The term *confirmation bias* describes the tendency for people to seek and notice only information that confirms what they already think—a case of people "hearing what they want to hear" and "seeing what they want to see," even when contradictory evidence is right in front of them. This obviously is not good for objective decision making.

The popular view was that the *Olympic*-class ships could survive any situation, so greater risks could be taken. Remember that people continued thinking with the same mental maps of the highest safety, even after *Olympic's* incidents. The first had been when a sudden reverse movement from *Olympic* made the ship collide with a smaller tug. The tug was seriously damaged, and it nearly sank. The owners sued White Star, but White Star counter sued and shifted the blame to the small-time operator of the tug because of lack of evidence.

Despite this, two weeks later, *Olympic* left New York with a record number of passengers.

The second was when *Olympic* collided with HMS *Hawke*, causing serious damage and making her unseaworthy. *Olympic* was headed out of Southampton with 13,000 passengers, who had to be unloaded when the crossing was canceled. This was very bad news for White Star.

Even so, they simply did not update their thinking after the collisions *Olympic* experienced. The belief that the *Olympic*-class ships were unsinkable had become so ingrained that any evidence that did not support their preconceptions did not seem to register.

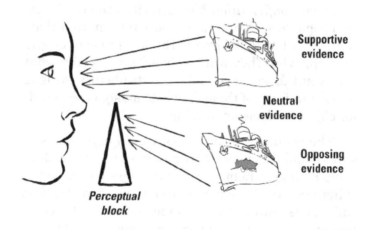

Supportive evidence

Neutral evidence

Opposing evidence

Perceptual block

Changing Circumstances

The *Hawke* incident had a big impact on White Star. No insurance was paid because *Olympic* was deemed at fault, so they could not recover the cost of repairs from the British Navy. There was also a knock-on effect on the work for Titanic.

Olympic would be out of service for at least eight weeks, which had a big financial consequence for White Star, and the priority had to be to get *Olympic* fixed and up and running as quickly as possible. The only place big enough to carry out the repairs was the dry dock in Belfast, which was used by Titanic at the time. *Olympic's* repair costs were 17% of the original cost to build her. As the insurance did not cover this incident, White Star was left with a big financial burden.

Managing Expectations

To accommodate this unfortunate turn of events, White Star rescheduled *Titanic's* maiden voyage from March 30 to April 10, 1912, with an announcement in the *London Times*. The negative publicity around this was damaging to White Star's credibility, especially with first-class passengers who would have to rearrange their calendars—something not easy to do for the world's movers and shakers. Ismay was very unhappy about this, as his focus was on making this the most important social event of 1912. He already had the problem of trying to upstage the hugely successful *Olympic's* maiden voyage.

Getting Back on Track—But at What Cost?

Even though the maiden voyage date was changed to give a few extra days, this hardly made up for the months of delay caused by *Olympic's* crash, not to mention the additional changes Ismay demanded. The pressure was on to meet the deadline, so they increased the workforce from 14,000 to more than 17,000. During the final month, they had three shifts running so work could continue through the night.

They were a remarkably efficient and dedicated workforce and, as a result, completed the work on Titanic so the deadline set for the maiden voyage would be met. However, it meant that they had less than one day of sea trials compared with *Olympic*, which had four weeks of extensive sea trials.

Their persistent belief in the ship's safety combined with commercial pressures meant they overlooked, or conveniently filtered out, the risks of Titanic missing full sea trials. Normally, the four weeks of trials meant that any final tweaks could be made, but White Star was prepared to sign the ship off solely based on their history with Harland and Wolff and *Olympic's* track record. They treated the two ships as identical and, because *Olympic* had already been in service, considered no need to go through extensive sea trials again. However, not only were the ships now structurally different because of the many changes made to Titanic, but there was also the fact that the crew would need time to get used to operating Titanic.

The Board of Trade surveyor must also have held the perception that these ships were invincible, as Titanic was issued a safety certificate after just half a day of sea trials.

Coping with Change

Where there is much pressure to meet a deadline, it's easy to take a narrow view and focus only on time. Change needs to be fully acknowledged as it occurs, so its consequences can be assessed from a variety of viewpoints. This can only happen effectively when a culture exists that allows team members to question decisions in a safe environment. Conforming to a single view means we will only see what we want to see and fail to address the real consequences of change.

Key points to consider for your projects:

- Do you have a change control process, and who is involved in the decision making?

- In what ways are different perspectives taken into account when assessing changes?

- How are your team members encouraged to express their views and concerns?

- How and when are changes in the project communicated to your customers?

- When you face conflicting information and opinions, is each idea examined with an open mind and with equal rigor?

- What preconceptions are held by the group?

- Are diverse opinions welcomed?

CHAPTER 6

Teams and Tensions

"Coming together is a beginning. Keeping together is progress. Working together is success."

—Henry Ford

A leader's role is critical in establishing effective teams. Initially, a team is just a collection of different people pulled together for a purpose. In this case, the purpose was the maiden voyage of Titanic—a project in itself. It was a unique event, as the crossing would never again be maiden. It was critical to the future of White Star that it was successful, which meant creating a magnificent, luxurious experience for the passengers, the like of which had never been seen before. Speed was not the issue.

The team was pulled together very quickly, as they had very little time to get ready, get up to speed, and operate effectively in a new environment. It is important to remember that each team member brings with them their own ideas and perspectives about what is expected from them and from others. They will have fundamental questions about what their objective is, how they will work together, and how they will carry out their duties. At this point, they look to the leader to provide clear direction and answers to these questions.

Setting up the Teams

This was a huge undertaking in itself. There were about 900 team members on the voyage: 475 stewards, bellboys, maids, and housekeepers and 320 mechanics, firemen, stokers, trimmers, greasers, and coal porters. That seems most of the team accounted for—oh, yes, and 83 mariners trained and capable of sailing the vessel!

The crew was organized into three main categories:

- **The senior team.** This was made of the captain and the officers. They were all employed full time, so they had preparation time before the voyage.

- **The maiden voyage support team from Harland and Wolff.** They would stand beside the operations staff and note any unfinished work and solve problems, either as they arose or noting them for when the ship returned to Belfast. This "snagging" should have been thoroughly covered during the sea trials, but that did not happen. The naval architect Andrews led this group.

- **The operations crew.** They would enable the ship to function as a floating luxury hotel and to navigate safely through the Atlantic waters. This was a new team, mostly hired just before sailing. They were only paid once the ship was out at sea, so no land-based preparation time was scheduled.

The overall team organization was hierarchical with, for example, seven engineers per watch supervising the work of more than ninety firemen, trimmers, and greasers. In addition, there were always three deck officers on duty per watch.

Improving Team Effectiveness

Time was very tight for the team leaders to pull their teams together and get them up and running. People need to know their duties and what is expected from them. They are also getting to know the lie of the land and one another. Rollin and Christine Glaser (1992) identified five elements that contribute to a team's productivity:

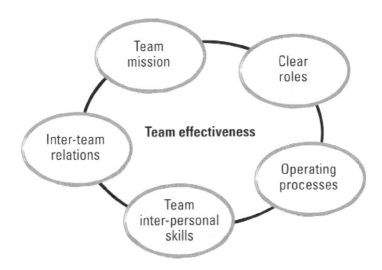

Team mission

The team needs a shared purpose or reason for
coming together. In this case, it is about achieving a
successful maiden voyage, which was what they all
worked toward. Within this, each team needs to be
clear on their objective and their contribution to the
overall mission. A strong sense of purpose among the
team motivates them to keep focused and organize
their work around their goal.

Leading up to the maiden voyage, there were
only five days of preparation time. To make the
situation worse, there was a coal strike that, if it had
continued just a few days longer, would most likely
have canceled the scheduled sailing on April 10.
White Star was forced to buy coal from other ships,
and in the process, other passengers transferred
to Titanic. The crew worked extremely hard to get
Titanic ready, as there was extreme pressure to set
sail as planned.

The White Star publicity machine had ensured
that the world was watching, and many journalists
were to sail with Titanic to cover the event. More
time could have been spent on focusing the teams
around the importance of their mission, to increase
motivation and bring everyone together.

Clearly defined roles

The teams consisted of many specialist domains,
each responsible for its areas. There were several
levels of support roles such as lookouts who would
be in the crow's nest, on-duty officers and crew
on the bridge, and radio operators in the wireless
room. Secondary support staff included the safety

officer (plotting positions of icebergs, currents, and weather systems), the navigation officer (plotting the position of the ship and maintaining the course) and specialized technical positions (such as the carpenter and the ship's doctor). The first and second officers and the captain provided the next level of support. Andrews and his team briefed the heads of departments, showed crew members how to operate things, and resolved any problems that occurred.

The White Star management team was highly experienced in ship operation, yet there were differences here because of the new technologies used and the sheer scale of the operation. For example, the radio operators were from Marconi and did not fall under the normal chain of command on the ship. We will see that the reporting lines were either not made clear to them, or they were not even considered.

Operating processes

Operating processes are essential for mapping how teams will get their work done and providing clear and efficient processes for escalating issues and making decisions. If team processes are set up clearly at the start, progress will be easier and time and energy will not be wasted on trying to work out how to deal with specific issues.

Over the first two days of the maiden voyage, Titanic received eight warnings reporting ice, icebergs, and ice floes. Sadly, the radio operators only sporadically relayed these ice warnings to the bridge because they were preoccupied with the flood of outgoing commercial radio messages and congratulatory incoming messages. In the thirty-six hours between leaving Southampton and the collision, Titanic received and sent 250 passenger telegrams. As Marconi company employees, the operators were contracted primarily to relay personal messages and were paid for each commercial radio message sent. Unfortunately, there were no procedures to prioritize messages, so a telegram to friends in New York could have a greater priority over any warning messages. The lack of information about procedures combined with their lack of knowledge of a ship's operations created a serious oversight.

During any new venture, there will be initial teething problems, so specific operating processes for this maiden voyage should have been thought about and communicated. It isn't sensible to try to apply generic processes that have worked elsewhere to a unique situation during transition or change.

Interpersonal relationships

Teams operate best when members can share opinions, discuss differences, clarify priorities, and reach agreements. To achieve these things, they need to be comfortable communicating with one another. However, in high-pressure situations, individual stress levels can rise, and there is a tendency to focus more on the tasks than the people aspects. Whether tasks are completed and agreements hold depends on the level of interactions taking place. Interpersonal issues among team members can be uncomfortable and get in the way of achieving the task. In this case, Captain Smith made last minute changes to the senior officers for the maiden voyage, which would have affected the team dynamics, leaving the officers involved little time to adjust.

William Murdoch had originally been assigned to Titanic as chief officer, but at the last minute, he was told to step aside to allow Henry Wilde, the chief officer from *Olympic*, to take this role. Murdoch then took the role of first officer. The knock-on effect was that the original first officer then became second officer, making the second officer Blair redundant. He was asked to leave the ship. Apparently, the change was reasonable because Wilde's experience with *Olympic* would be invaluable on the maiden voyage. However, this was done in such a last-minute rush that when Blair packed to leave the ship, he took the key to the lockers with him—we presume unintentionally. These lockers were the responsibility of the second officer and held the binoculars for the lookout crew. This meant the lookout crew had no access to binoculars for the voyage and could not do their job. The cause of the missing key was due to a lack of clear processes for conducting the hand over when the reorganization occurred.

After leaving Southampton, the lookouts repeatedly reported that they didn't have binoculars, but nothing was done, even though the officers could have shared their own. The lookouts became resentful because they did not have the tools they needed to work effectively, and the officers seemed very unwilling to cooperate with them. There would certainly have been a "them and us" mindset because of the large cultural divide between the officers and the lookouts, and they let this divide override the focus on their shared objective and their responsibility to achieve the outcome. Underlying this was also the perception that the ship was so safe they did not need to worry about problems.

Inter-team relations

This was a very large operation with many diverse teams, so cultural factors came into play too. The living conditions for the crew were basic, with about forty sleeping in a single dormitory. This was in complete contrast to the privileges the officers enjoyed. It seems that the officers did not have clear communication channels with the other crew members, which led to delayed communications or, worse still, important information not being relayed at all.

The organizational hierarchy was complex, with many teams and subteams. As the ship was so large, you could say some of them operated like virtual teams, as they would never have come into direct contact with many of their colleagues. The Marconi radio messaging team was particularly isolated and their managers were not even on the ship.

Teams cannot work in isolation when aiming to achieve a common goal. The Titanic teams made up a complex web of interrelated systems, each with a separate part to contribute but only able to be successful as part of the whole. However effective teams might be at addressing the previous four elements, they also need to pay attention to connecting with the other teams, for example in the case of the radio operators.

Managing the Stages of Team Development

It is common to see barriers to communication and tensions appear when attention has not been paid, either to how the team was established or to the different team dynamics as they go through change. The Titanic teams did not have clear leadership to help them establish sound team working practices or the time to focus on this.

Tuckman (1965) described how teams go through stages of development as they work toward becoming effective.

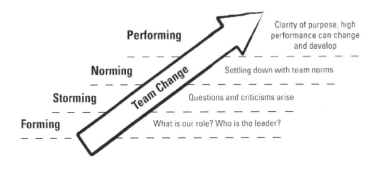

Forming

This is the time of questions and initial niceties. Team members need basic questions answered about what their role is, what will be achieved, and how they will work together. They look for direction from the leader so their questions can be answered. A lack of direction and unclear operating processes can lead to serious problems.

Storming

The team moves beyond the initial politeness and members are ready to question and challenge the decisions made and how they are expected to work. They might struggle for some control, and there can be signs of conflict, tensions, and disagreement that distract them from getting the work done. They look for support and direction from the leader to help them through this stage.

Norming

This is when the team settles into a normal way of working. Fundamental questions have been answered; people know what they are doing; and tensions have been dealt with sufficiently to allow a focus on the task. As challenges arise, team members are more confident about dealing with them. There is less need for direction from the leader, who continues to provide appropriate levels of support. Further challenges and questions might take the team back to the Forming or Storming stage. If teams show a pattern of moving back and forth between the Norming and Storming stages, it indicates that there might be some underlying issues that are not being dealt with. Any change to the team will also upset the dynamics and send the team back to an earlier stage. The last-minute changes to the officer roles before Titanic sailed could have had this impact.

Performing

This is when teams are well established and work at a high level. They learn how to make the most of one another's strengths and can be flexible, adapting easily to changing needs. This was the case with the team at Harland and Wolff during the design and construction phases. Harland and Wolff used their regular workforce, and the teams had been working together for a long time, using established work processes in a reasonably stable environment with strong longstanding relationships.

This is the stage when you get cohesion among the team and "group think" such that the team starts to think in the same way without knowing it— and tending to jump at decisions without sufficient exploration of alternatives.

The problems that occurred during the maiden voyage indicate that the teams simply failed to work well together, this effected how they communicated and how well the processes worked.

Balancing the Needs of the Task, Team, and Individuals

We have seen that a leader must keep multiple dimensions in sight.

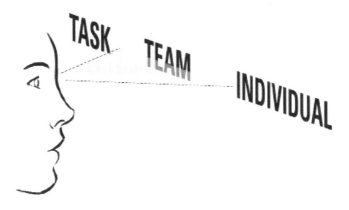

- **Task focus**. What is the task? Clearly, they were under much pressure. They just had a few days to get the ship prepared and be ready for the maiden voyage. There was much to do, and on top of this, there was the coal strike, meaning additional logistics to deal with to get the coal from other ships and more shuffling of crew members. It was so important for them to meet the deadline, and their focus was very much on getting ready for this date.

- **Team focus**. They were experienced in running ships, so they knew what crew would be needed. There were many teams to get on board in a short time. However, due to the tight schedules, there was not enough focus on thinking about getting these teams established and used to working with each other. The elements described above were not thought about fully, as there just was no time. The team dynamics from changing roles were not considered, either. Captain Smith could have given this more consideration.

- **Individual focus**. Teams are made of individuals, and their needs come with them. Everyone will have their reasons for joining the team, whether for job security, a regular paycheck, or because they are interested in the challenge and being part of the adventure. When individual needs can be met with the project goals, the team will be far more effective and much more motivated. Captain Smith might have considered what Ismay's needs were and how his expectations could be managed.

When all three areas are given balanced attention, the result is that the teams will be much more effective in working together and achieving their outcome. Due to the time pressures and the rush to meet the scheduled sailing date, the focus on *Titanic* was very much on the task. In the next chapter, we will see the problems arising from not maintaining a balanced focus and neglecting the team and individual areas.

Key points to consider for your projects:

- In which stage of team development is your team currently?

- What support do they need from you or the team leader?

Using a scale of 1 to 10 (1 being poor, 10 being very good), how would you rate your team on these factors:

- How clear are they on their purpose as a team?

- Do members understand what their role is and what is expected from them?

- Are they comfortable with how the team will work together, that is, the standard processes for raising issues and making decisions?

- Can team members share opinions openly and discuss their differences with one another?

- What is the level of connecting and communicating with other teams around them?

CHAPTER 7

Communication and Conflict

*"The biggest problem with communication is
the illusion that it has happened."*
—George Bernard Shaw

Conflict is natural when diverse groups of people work on projects. It occurs when there are disagreements or differences in goals, thoughts, or emotions among people and groups.

Misunderstandings and a poor communication flow are major causes of conflict, so it is just as important to put effort into ensuring the internal teams communicate well as it is managing communications with external parties and stakeholders. Knowing the barriers to communication can help avoid the typical pitfalls that occur. It is critical for managers and leaders to recognize and deal with conflict if they will be successful in achieving their aims.

The world's press paid close attention to the maiden voyage's success, putting additional pressure on the operations team. If you combine this type of pressure with the fact that it was a new environment, and they were new to working with one another, you have a perfect recipe for tension and conflict. The way relationships and conflicts were managed on *Titanic* was a key factor in what followed.

Communicating Inside and Outside

In the buildup to *Titanic's* maiden voyage, Ismay did a superb job with marketing and getting the right levels of information out to the public at the right times. This resulted in widespread interest in the ships on both sides of the Atlantic. However, little effort was put into communication on board the ship, which would have helped avoid the barriers to communication that led to unnecessary bottlenecks and conflicts.

There is a danger of communication overload if people are bombarded with too much information that is not timely and relevant to them. It is important for everyone to be clear on how to decide what is important and relevant and what is not. Otherwise, there is a risk that important information will be missed, just as it was with the two radio operators. They were overwhelmed with telegram messages and the ice warnings, but they did not know how to prioritize them. Or rather, they prioritized the messages based on the criteria that they were paid for each commercial message sent, which was clearly different from the criteria Captain Smith would have used.

Barriers to communication include:

- **Lack of subject knowledge**—This can get in the way of shared understanding and lead to misconceptions and wrong decisions being made. Had the two radio operators from Marconi had more shipping knowledge, they would have appreciated the importance of the iceberg messages.

- **Cultural differences**—Cultural divides can be deeply ingrained unconsciously. There was a big cultural difference between the officers and the lookout crew, which acted as a barrier to collaborative working and open communication.

- **Organizational culture**—The culture they operated in was very hierarchical with top-down lines of command. In this environment, the lookout crew would not have been expected to challenge the decisions of the officers. They could not do much about the senior officers not making binoculars available to them.

- **Perceptions**—As we have already seen in chapter three, people create their own perceptions based on the unique filters they run and the mental shortcuts they make, which means they make assumptions about who they will communicate with and how the message will be received.

A serious failing occurred in the way the ice detection test was reported on the ship. The ice detection test was usually carried out by testing the temperature of the seawater frequently when approaching ice fields, as a noticeable temperature change is a good indicator that large ice floes are near. The test involves drawing seawater from over the side of the ship with a bucket and testing the temperature of this water with a thermometer.

One of *Titanic's* passengers noticed a mariner filling a bucket with tap water and asked why he was doing that. The mariner explained that he was supposed to take the seawater's temperature, but he complained that the rope was not long enough to reach the sea! The ice detection test was worthless. This mariner could communicate what he was doing to the passenger yet didn't think he could tell his senior officers. His perception was probably that he would have been reprimanded for the problem, so he did not bother to tell them.

Had the mariner thought that it was safe to report this problem or that doing so would make a difference, he most likely would have done this. His perceptions influenced his decision not to report the problem. By knowing these types of barriers, leaders can look for potential problems and can choose to do something about them.

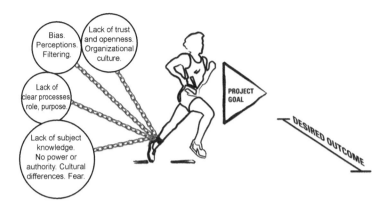

Balancing Power and Authority

When thinking about communication and the potential for conflict, it is useful to consider how power and authority play across the team. Power is the ability to get others to do the work you want them to do through influencing them. Authority, on the other hand, is the formal power given to people because of their hierarchical position—a position that gives them the right to command or deliver orders. On *Titanic*, there was enough opportunity for a clash of the two.

As a show of confidence, Ismay promoted Captain Smith to commodore of the White Star Fleet. This was a great honor for him and enhanced his reputation. Captain Smith was already quite a celebrity. He was known as the "Millionaire's Captain," and people often chose to sail on ships especially because he was the captain. Being given this promotion to be commodore of the White Star Fleet raised his standing even further.

As these ships were so important to White Star, Ismay decided to be on board for the maiden voyage. This was supportive from a project sponsor perspective, but it immediately changed the power dynamic on the ship. Ismay was a very influential character who wielded much power, and this could clash with the idea of the captain holding ultimate authority and responsibility. So, although Smith had the legitimate authority as captain, Ismay would have a big influence on the decisions made. This *Titanic* voyage would be Captain Smith's last before retiring, so he likely wanted to avoid any conflict with Ismay who had made him Admiral of the Fleet.

Moving the Goal Posts

The rush to meet the sailing schedule meant there was no time to open the ship to the public before the voyage, so Ismay had lost a publicity opportunity. *Olympic* had received so much attention that Ismay was worried about *Titanic* becoming an also-ran and not receiving the fanfare she deserved. Continued publicity was essential to White Star's future success. He decided he could make the case that *Titanic* had benefited as the second ship and position it as a big improvement over the *Olympic*. The size and luxury angle had already been promoted widely when *Olympic* was launched, so he needed a new angle.

It occurred to Ismay that by beating *Olympic's* best crossing time, he could market *Titanic* as a superior liner. In reality, there was no technical advancement or improvement, and Ismay was at this point changing the team's shared goal and success criteria for the maiden voyage project!

Just before *Titanic* sailed, he put a very small shipping announcement into the *New York Times* to

94

be printed on Monday, April 15. This announced that *Titanic* would arrive on Tuesday night rather than the published schedule of Wednesday morning. He did this without communicating with the captain and the officers, giving them no opportunity to question his decision. This was a turning point, as this was where Ismay usurped the control of the ship from Captain Smith—before *Titanic* even set off. The first signs of the lack of clarity between their roles appeared, even before the maiden voyage started.

Recognizing Different Conditions that Lead to Conflict

By the time *Titanic* sailed, it was evident there were incompatible goals and poor communication— conflict was inevitable. Filley (1975) identified several conditions that can lead to conflict if not addressed. Among these are no clearly defined roles and inconsistent goals across teams. Captain Smith's goal was to complete the maiden voyage for *Titanic* as planned and ensure the guests were well looked after. Ismay became distracted by trying to get an attention-grabbing result by beating *Olympic's* best crossing time. They had different goals in mind.

When one group depends on another that has its own priorities, this can also lead to problems. The lookouts needed binoculars, but they depended on the officers to provide them. A divide can easily occur between different specialist areas where each has its own viewpoint, language, and ways of doing things. Unresolved prior conflicts will tend to linger and even minor conflicts can spiral into much more intense conflict if they are not dealt with. Generally, the longer things are left unresolved, the worse they get.

Encouraging Some Conflict

It is important to remember that conflict can be a good thing as well as negative, depending on its impact on the team's performance. Minor conflicts, if not managed effectively, can lead to major conflicts and unwanted consequences. Carlisle's challenge about the lifeboats could have been a very positive intervention; instead, it led to his resignation.

When there is trust and respect among team members, healthy conflict is very beneficial. It encourages the team to have a rethink and see things from different perspectives, drawing out hidden assumptions and creating better solutions.

If there are very low levels of conflict, the organization might be very unresponsive to change and lack new ideas. However, if the conflict levels are too high, it can hinder performance drastically, as the environment will be too chaotic and disruptive. Leaders need to keep a close eye on the situation.

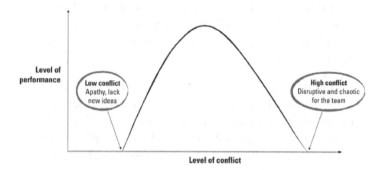

Resolving Conflict

The way conflict is managed can have a significant impact on a project's outcome, so being able to manage conflict is a vital skill for leaders; they should expect conflict and prepare for it. Part of this preparation involves understanding the situation around them and looking for the possible sources of conflict. Often people are uncomfortable with conflict and hope that it will go away if ignored, but the best way to deal with this is to confront it to surface the real problems.

Three main steps for managing conflicts are:

- **Preparing for the conflict**—assume it is inevitable and plan for it.

- **Facing the conflict**—don't try to sweep the problems under the carpet; surface them, analyze the situation, and find the causes.

- **Resolving the conflict**—look for a positive outcome that offers a win-win alternative.

Blake and Mouton (1964) presented five general techniques for resolving conflict:

- **Withdrawing (or avoiding)**—This involves avoiding, pulling out or drawing back to avoid any possible confrontation. It is a refusal to deal with the situation. It can allow time to pause when a cooling-off period might be needed, but it won't solve the problem. Although Captain Smith attempted to share some earlier ice warnings with Ismay, he did not address continuing to travel at high speed.

97

- **Smoothing (or accommodating)**—
  This emphasizes the common ground and
  avoids any discussion of the issues that might
  cause divisions. This appeasing approach
  might work in the short term but fails to
  provide a longer-term solution. Captain
  Smith seemed more interested in keeping
  things amicable with Ismay.

- **Forcing**—This implies imposing one
  viewpoint at the expense of another, creating
  a win-lose situation. It can be used when
  there is no common ground for bargaining or
  when time is critical, and a quick decision is
  needed.

- **Compromising**—This helps find a middle
  ground acceptable to all, based on considering
  all the issues and reaching a solution
  that to some degree satisfies both parties.
  Unfortunately, it might mean that neither
  party is entirely happy with the outcome.

- **Collaborating (or problem solving)**—This
  requires discussing problems openly and
  fully collaborating to search for a solution
  genuinely good for everyone involved. It
  is best used for situations that are too
  important to be compromised and when the
  positions of the different players are at odds.

Forcing, smoothing, and withdrawing are
generally not good for addressing the real cause
of the conflict. Compromise might not be effective,
either, as not all parties might get what they really
wanted. Generally, the most effective approach is

collaborating or problem solving; this approach aims for a win-win result.

Choosing an Effective Resolution

Thomas and Kilmann (1976) point out that the effectiveness of these resolution methods depends on taking into account two other factors:

- Desire to satisfy oneself (concern for one's own views)

- Desire to satisfy others (concern for others' views)

They believe that avoiding or withdrawing correspond to not being interested in meeting your needs or the needs of others. Accommodating or smoothing indicates being more interested in appeasing the other party at the expense of meeting your needs. Compromising corresponds to a medium level of desire to satisfy both others and yourself. Collaboration or problem solving reflects a strong interest in wanting to satisfy your needs as well as those of others, and forcing is an urgent need to get what you want with little desire to meet the needs of others.

Which conflict resolution approach will be best depends on:

- Type and relative importance of the conflict for you

- Time pressures

- Positions of the players involved

- Relative emphasis on goals as opposed to relationships

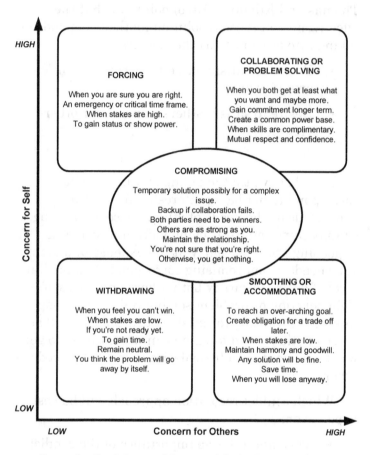

Captain Smith would most likely have put the relationship with Ismay above the need to worry about their disagreement.

Had the leaders of *Titanic* thought about the conflicts that could occur and dealt with the situation, the disaster might not have happened.

Cooperating to Overcome Problems

The crew did not work as a team and communicate with one another. The right leadership direction could have helped the team feel empowered and motivated, increasing their sense of ownership and responsibility. The mariner taking the water temperature tests needed to decide about what action to take and, in that hierarchical environment, would have needed very clear instructions about how to escalate issues. The *Titanic* crew had neither the open, cooperative style of working that would have enabled them to share what was going on, make decisions, and take action, nor did they have clear direction about what to do when there was a problem.

In a stable environment such as business as usual operations, there has been time to test and establish normal working practices that would include clear escalation routes. However, in a time of transition, those practices have not been established, so there is a need for more flexibility and temporary structures, enabling a more cooperative mode of working with open communication flows.

Empowerment is one of those things that people and organizations like the sound of, but typically, they don't follow through with the actions to make it a reality. It is an easy word to say, but making it happen takes work and courage.

Key points to consider for your projects:

- What are the potential barriers to communication among your team and stakeholders?

- What factors could be playing a part in causing conflict?

- What is the level of trust and respect among the project team?

- What are the power dynamics in play among your key stakeholders?

- Is everyone clear on the priorities?

- Are there any issues with conflicting priorities that need to be addressed?

- How comfortable are you with conflict?

- When resolving conflict, which approaches are you most comfortable with, and which would be a stretch for you?

CHAPTER 8

Risks and Reframing

*"What you see and hear depends a good deal
on where you are standing; it also depends on
what sort of person you are."*
—C. S. Lewis

C learly, even though they managed to meet the date for the maiden voyage with apparent success, all the while, behavioral issues simmered under the surface. These were not so apparent to anyone because no one paid attention to this side of things. As the project progressed, the overconfidence in the safety of *Titanic*, the level of compromises, the lack of challenge to key decisions, and the communication issues emerging led to a gradual buildup of risk.

There are three key points to consider when deciding what to do about risks:

- How likely is it that something will occur?
- If it does occur, what will be the knock-on effect, or in other words the impact?

- Is this knock-on effect worth worrying about and, if so, what should be done about it?

Thinking about these three factors together will help determine whether something should be done. The actions you choose to take to address a risk could help reduce either the likelihood of it happening or the impact it will have it if does.

Recognizing Risks

A person's attitude to uncertainty affects how they respond to situations. It also affects whether they see things as risky and what they choose to do about it. The key stakeholders were innovative and entrepreneurial, and that they were prepared to embark on such an ambitious project shows they were comfortable taking risks.

If the key players had felt there was any uncertainty about *Titanic's* safety, they would have put more effort into thinking about the risks and dealing with them. However, it was quite the opposite. The positive filters set early in the project meant there was a continuing confidence that *Titanic* was unsinkable, so how could there be any risks? Less focus on risks meant that fewer risks were identified, which in turn reinforced the view that the venture was not risky and led to more complacency in the way risks were managed.

Ismay was certainly prone to spotting what he felt were opportunities and overplaying their importance. Others might have seen these things as threats or serious challenges, but Ismay did not seem to notice risks at all. He decided to race

Titanic across the Atlantic and try to beat *Olympic's* crossing time. All he could see through his filters was the opportunity to grab headlines and generate more revenue.

Identifying and Assessing the Impact of Risk

The shortened sea trials were not seen as a risk, nor were the limited tests that formed *Titanic's* final inspection at Queenstown, the last port before the main Atlantic crossing. The belief in *Titanic's* invincibility was so strong that it even affected the Board of Trade inspectors, who allowed shortcuts in the final safety inspections.

As part of this final readiness check, a lifeboat drill was carried out in front of the inspectors. During the drill, only two of the twenty lifeboats were lowered, and they did not reach the water, so the test was never fully completed. The drill outlined that it took 8 to 10 well-trained men to prepare and lower a lifeboat, but they did not consider what would be required if all the lifeboats had to be launched at once—a challenging task for the small team of 83 trained mariners in the 900 strong crew. This final test in Queenstown was inadequate and highlighted that the whole approach was still influenced by the belief that little could go wrong.

Risk can also be seen as an opportunity, in which case, you would look to increase the likelihood of it happening and try to leverage more from it. Having spotted an opportunity to get publicity for *Titanic* by beating *Olympic's* crossing time, Ismay acted to increase the likelihood of it happening and asked for more boilers to be lit during the voyage to make the ship go faster.

A certainty for *Titanic* was that there would be icebergs and possibly storms in the Atlantic. The winter of 1911/12 had been exceptionally mild, and many icebergs had broken loose. The White Star team knew that the volume of ice spotted had increased because of the El Niño warming of the Pacific in 1911. The area was known as Iceberg Alley to the captain and the crew.

As the ice was certain to be present, Captain Smith decided to move the sailing path south by ten miles, which would avoid the most concentrated areas of ice, but would not affect the sailing time, and they would still arrive in New York as originally scheduled. So, interestingly, action was taken to avoid the ice, but they did not go further and think about what would happen if *Titanic* struck it.

Understanding Framing

The total confidence the *Titanic* team enjoyed continued throughout the maiden voyage. They still looked through a positively filtered view that framed everything they saw. In other words, they looked at everything within the context of *Titanic's* complete invincibility.

The way we frame things helps us make sense of the information we have gathered and gives it meaning. We rely on this to understand what is occurring and decide what to do. Think of it as looking through a camera lens—we only see what is in this lens.

With a different lens, we might see something very different.

We do not look at something and then adapt our lens. Instead, we constantly look at the world through preset frames that allow us to make sense of the incoming messages. Framing is another mental shortcut to process information in set chunks. This can certainly be useful, but in the case of *Titanic*, it greatly influenced the team's attitude to risk. Framing affected both the identification of risks for the voyage and the way those risks were understood and dealt with.

Looking Beyond the Frame—Reframing

Through the wireless Marconigram, the captain and officers were made aware of the fate of a French liner *Niagara* that had run into ice. They knew the likelihood of this occurring at this time of year was high, and they believed that this could not affect *Titanic*, so there was nothing to worry about. The *Niagara* incident fell outside their frame, and they didn't focus on it.

However, Captain Smith handed the *Niagara* telegram to Ismay, probably to warn him not to keep pushing to increase the crossing speed. Ismay read it and then put it in his pocket. Witnesses say that he flaunted an iceberg warning received that day at dinner to show that these were of no concern. Ismay's view was very much framed around arriving a day early and the huge publicity and future revenue that would generate.

On the night of April 15, near Iceberg Alley, stars brightly illuminated the sky, and the sea was incredibly calm. There was a haze on the horizon created by the cold weather. These conditions made it difficult to outline the horizon as it merged with the sky. It was usual practice to post extra lookouts on the ship's bow, a great vantage point for ice, to which a telephone link ran from the bridge. Given all the warning signs, surprisingly, no extra lookouts were on duty that night. They must have thought that they would see anything in good time, given the excellent visibility, which is another example of how their overconfident views influenced their attitude to risk and the decisions made.

Multiple warning signs along the way were all overlooked. Five ice warnings had been received during the day, with three further warnings delivered to the bridge in the evening while Captain Smith dined with the guests.

Looking at one iceberg warning through a limited frame offers some information, but does not look like much of a problem. Changing the frame and piecing together all the ice-warning information would have indicated a giant ice field around eighty miles wide, directly ahead of them. This has a very different meaning, and understanding this would have changed everything.

As well as dealing with the daily detailed issues, it is important for leaders to zoom out and keep their eye on the bigger picture; otherwise, they won't "see the forest for the trees." In effect, this changes the frame to give a different meaning to the situation.

 Key points to consider for your projects:

- How do you feel about uncertainty and risk?

- How about your team, stakeholders, and the wider organization—what is their attitude to risk?

- What beliefs and assumptions could be getting in the way of how risks are handled?

- Practice looking through different frames and different angles to get multiple perspectives on a situation.

CHAPTER 9

Decisions and Disaster

"Facts do not cease to exist because they are ignored."
                                        —Aldous Huxley

D uring any venture, things are likely not to
go as planned, and leaders should expect
challenges and obstacles. Without a crystal
ball, the exact nature of these cannot be predicted,
but leaders should help their teams by preparing for
unexpected situations. The leader's role is to ensure
the team has agreed how issues will be handled
and how decisions will be made. This all needs to be
made clear right at the beginning of the project, not
amid a crisis.

Facing the Unexpected
Although icebergs were a known risk, no one
expected them to drift down as far south as they did.
The ship, at its maximum speed, raced through icy
still waters littered with small bergs and pieces of

ice. The lookouts, with no binoculars and a freezing wind hitting their eyes, tried to outline the horizon through the haze. It took them a while to make out the dark mass looming in front of them, so there was a delay before they telephoned this to the bridge.

An iceberg, dark and nearly invisible in the haze, had flipped. Once sure of their sighting, the lookouts notified the bridge with the infamous "Iceberg dead ahead". The chief duty officer calmly took the call, cut off the engines, and although he didn't manage to avoid contact with the ice, he prevented a head-on crash that could have demolished the first four compartments.

Two minutes later, as part of standard naval procedures, two damage assessment parties were sent to the front and midship to determine the extent of the damage. The first party returned in less than ten minutes and reported to Captain Smith that they found no major damage or flooding. Given their confidence in *Titanic's* safety, Captain Smith assumed the situation was not serious.

Making Decisions

At this point, Ismay rushed into making a decision without waiting to gather all the information. Making a decision is like problem solving. Gathering information and identifying options are critical steps toward effective decision making, and Ismay would have done well to wait to hear other views. In his mind, the assessment was now complete, even though the second party had not returned with their findings. He was keen to get *Titanic* moving again, and it seems that little negotiation occurred. He was a powerful figure, used to getting his way, and the chain of command on the ship between him and Captain Smith had already become very blurred. Ismay's urgency to continue created an unnecessary time pressure that led to a rushed decision and contributed to turning a critical situation into a catastrophe.

Considering Differing Perspectives

From Ismay's perspective, a distress call would pose a real problem, as it would shatter the marketing hype about the invincibility of the Olympic-class ships. For him, a far better option was to get the ship back to Halifax, away from New York and the world's press. He could then at least contain the news story, so it would be reported only as a minor incident. He could claim that *Titanic*, a lifeboat in itself with all the latest in emerging technologies, could save herself from a disaster. From his perspective, this was a much better alternative and the key driver for his decision.

He was so focused on saving White Star's and his own reputation, that it blinded him from sensibly exploring all the options. Captain Smith had passed Ismay a telegram containing an ice warning—it seems he wasn't prepared to challenge Ismay, but let him take on the ship's leadership. It was his last voyage, and perhaps understandably, he wanted to avoid any confrontation with the person who had promoted him to Commander of the Fleet.

Generating Multiple Options

According to Ismay, they seemed to have two options: continue and save face or send out a distress call. Considering only two options creates an either/or dilemma that is very limiting. Having more choices to work with gives you more room for maneuver and leads to better-quality decisions.

We must keep in mind that this was a highly stressful situation. It is tempting to rush into a decision, but the consequences of making a poor judgment are far too serious to shy away from, considering all the options available.

Here are some steps to follow when making decisions:

- **Define the problem**—What is the real problem? Gather all the facts, rather than just what is shouted about.

- **Analyze the problem**—Understand why it is happening—what are the causes? Test your findings. How quickly do you need to act before things get worse? Or is the situation stable?

- **Identify possible options**— shuttle between looking at detail and the bigger picture, and get multiple perspectives by asking different experts. Also include what would happen if you did nothing.

- **Analyze the options**—Assess the options and consider what would happen and what would not happen for each option.

- **Make a decision**—Make sure the decision is clear and communicated to everyone.

Titanic seemed stable, sitting snugly on the underwater ice shelf. Maybe with care, they could dislodge the ship with minimum damage.

Make a decision ⇧
Analyze the options ⇧
Identify possible options ⇧
Analyze the problem ⇧
Define the problem ⇧

Making Quality Decisions

Ten minutes after the collision, before the second assessment party had even returned, Ismay pushed to restart the ship and sail to Halifax. Captain Smith gave the order to sail forward "dead slow" and *Titanic* moved with a grinding noise.

When the second damage assessment party returned, which included the architect Andrews, they reported that the mailroom was flooded, and the ship was doomed. Smith conferred with Andrews and the officers and decided that the ship should gradually stop. When making important decisions under pressure, it is very useful to have a guiding set of principles or values on which to fall back. For instance, *Californian* was sailing north of *Titanic* and similarly avoided a collision with an ice shelf but immediately decided to stop for the night. The Leyland Line, owners of *Californian*, had stated principles that a captain's first responsibilities were to his ship and his passengers and that "no supposed

115

gain in expediting or saving of time on the voyage is to be purchased at the risk of accident."

Clear values to work with form the basis of trust and empowerment across an organization. Captain Stanley was empowered to make decisions and did not need to contact his headquarters for permission to pull up for the night. Neither was there any fear about the consequences of this decision. It was a straightforward decision for him to make based on clear principles that had been agreed beforehand.

By contrast, the situation on *Titanic* was very different. Even though Captain Smith should have had the authority to make the final decision, this was not so. They did not have an agreed decision-making process in place; it came about as the situation evolved. The decision was very much driven by Ismay, and the commercial pressures White Star faced heavily influenced his motivation— not the most effective way to proceed.

Key points to consider for your projects:

- How do you and your team make decisions? Is this process clear to everyone?

- Are decisions made objectively and by involving the right people?

- Always consider more than two options to avoid an either/or dilemma.

- Are time pressures blinding you from sensibly exploring all the options?

- What other factors might influence the decision-making process?

CHAPTER 10

Crisis and Collision

"Nothing is inevitable until it happens."
—A. J. P. Taylor

T hey now had a full-blown crisis on their hands. This was a time for acting quickly and with courage to manage the critical situation. Strong leadership was required to ensure people knew what to do.

In a crisis, time is a leader's enemy. When a crisis looms, normal daily operating processes need to be suspended and quick decisions made to reassure everyone that he or she is in able hands. People need to know that their leaders:

- Understand that there is a problem
- Take it seriously
- Are taking steps to address the problem

Captain Smith finally recognized that the situation was hopeless. Had he accepted the severity of their position earlier, it would probably have been recoverable, but this delay in acting turned out to be tragic. It was about sixty-five minutes after the collision that he finally gave orders to uncover the lifeboats and get the passengers and crew ready on deck.

Responding in the Golden Hour

Crisis management professionals speak of the Golden Hour of crisis response, using a metaphor from emergency medicine. If critically injured people are treated in one hour, their chance of survival increases significantly. The same applies to crisis management—a quick response will always get better results.

Although the captain and a few officers knew the extent of the damage, and they had accepted that the ship was sinking, there was still no "abandon ship" command or formal declaration of a disaster given.

Falling into the Trap of Denial

Unfortunately, many leaders can be slow to respond appropriately and fall into a common crisis trap—denial. The idea of *Titanic* sinking had been unthinkable for them. They had failed to explore this possibility and the risk of hitting an iceberg had not been acknowledged. The shock of the unthinkable happening meant that a period of denial was inevitable—a very strong reason to be open-minded and explore potential risks before any happen! The key to success is to pass through this denial stage quickly staying calm and moving forward in a way that offers energy and inspiration to the teams involved.

Holding on to Normality

The crew carried out orders to launch the lifeboats but, for a long time, doubted that anything serious would happen. Most passengers were unaware of the disaster, and the lifeboats were filled on a first-come, first-served basis from the top decks, mainly with first- and second-class passengers. Although each lifeboat had a capacity of sixty-five people, only twenty-seven people were lowered into the first, and the first eight lifeboats left half-empty.

The normalcy bias refers to a type of response that people can show when they face a disaster. They are strongly biased to believing that normality will continue as it always has, and they fail to accept either the possibility of disaster or its impact. It is very similar to denial and means that people are much less prepared and are reluctant to accept there is a problem, even when they are in the midst of it. They still hold on to the idea that it is impossible for this to occur, and they tend to interpret warnings optimistically, looking for any inconsistencies which would justify them thinking the situation was less than serious.

Even when they start to see that the disaster is happening, the normalcy bias can cause people to underestimate the effects of it drastically. They believe that everything will be all right, even when the evidence indicates a very serious situation.

Communicating Openly and Giving Direction

To manage a crisis, there needs to be open and consistent communication to everyone involved. This is a highly, emotionally charged situation and people will be under immense stress or in denial. To get a message understood in this climate, communications need to be repeated. Under these circumstances, normal operational procedures will not work. Temporary procedures need to be put in place, communicated, and made clear to everyone.

Even once he knew the full extent of the disaster, Captain Smith did not communicate this to either the crew or the passengers on board. This increased the confusion, particularly among the crew. For example, the engine room sent some engineers to the boat deck, but the bridge sent them back down to the engine room.

Several factors might have contributed to the poor communications:

- The ship had very limited communication capabilities, with no public-address system.

- Important information was communicated to passengers by word of mouth, the crew knocking on each cabin door, and making announcements in the common rooms. This would have taken hours considering there were hundreds of cabins.

- The crew didn't have accurate information on the situation, so mixed information was passed to passengers. Captain Smith believed in the safety systems of the ship and might have found the architect's verdict very difficult to accept because everything seemed so normal in the first hour. He acted as if the situation were "business as usual"—showing signs of denial.

- The captain realized that the carrying capacity of the lifeboats was inadequate, with only enough room for about half the estimated 2,223 people on board. There were no mass communications to keep things calm and to allow the lifeboats to be filled in an orderly way when the timing was right. The ship's hierarchical structure and segregation of classes meant that first-class passengers had the best access to the boats.

- The captain feared widespread panic. With room in the lifeboats for only half the people on board, widespread panic could have broken out.

Captain Smith knew he could save the maximum number of lives by loading only those fortunate enough to reach the boats. So, he might have avoided informing all the passengers, specifically those in third class.

Acting with Resolve

When there is a serious problem to deal with, a leader needs to act with conviction. We all can do this; when it is a matter close to our hearts and important enough, we step up to the mark. The key is to recognize there is a problem and decide to act. In situations such as this, there is no guaranteed right solution, and there isn't the luxury of time to ponder whether you should. It takes courage and preparation to take risks.

Key points to consider for your projects:

- Is there a clear escalation route for reporting issues?

- Is there an agreed procedure with the key people nominated to deal with serious problems?

- Are suitable communication procedures in place, which enable the right people to be contacted promptly and effectively?

- Is there a suitable risk-management process in place to identify potential problems in the first place?

Conclusion

That *Titanic* could sink was not even considered. We have explored some issues that directly contributed to the disaster—the perception set about the ship's safety and the way this was continually reinforced through filters and biases. We have looked at how people started to believe their own hype and the effects of changing goals and requirements. Power dynamics were important, with just one person's view dominating and little consideration given to wider requirements and perspectives. No one succeeded in challenging Ismay, and the culture didn't encourage anyone to try.

The crew was made from several teams, but their roles, the way they worked together, and the alignment of their goals just hadn't been considered. When it came to the crunch and things started to go wrong, there was no process in place and no clear direction to deal with the crisis, and communication was poor.

It was not a lack of engineering excellence or the iceberg that sank *Titanic*; it was a failure to realize the importance of those communication and leadership problems that could have made it successful.

Turning Lessons into Action

"The world can only be grasped by action, not contemplation."
—Jacob Bronowski

Learning is only useful when it can be turned into action, so you see a change in the results you get. There are many lessons to take from this book, and I invite you to review the different topics when you feel the need. For now, to get you started on your journey, here are three main areas to consider:

- What are the beliefs and assumptions reinforced in your environment? Ask yourself and your team what would happen if these were not true. Would you do anything differently on your project?

- Will the project deliver what is required and meet your key stakeholders' expectations? If there is a gap, make sure you highlight it and let people know why.

- What are the team dynamics, and how well do team members work together? What else might they need to help overcome any barriers to communication?

Every journey starts with a single step, and you have already taken the first step by reading this book. I hope you have found fresh insights and useful models along the way, and the important thing now is to put these ideas into practice. Just one small step at a time is all it takes to start seeing a difference. So, over to you now, and I wish you well on your journey...

Titanic Lessons in Project Leadership

Bibliography

Adair, John. *Effective Team Building: How to Make a Winning Team.* London, UK: Pan MacMillan, 2009.

Association for Project Management. *APM Body of Knowledge 5th Edition.* 2006.

Blake, Robert Rogers, and Jane Srygley Mouton. *The Managerial Grid III: A New Look at the Classic that Has Boosted Productivity and Profits for Thousands of Corporations Worldwide.* Foley, Alabama: Gulf Publishing, 1985.

Cameron, Esther, and Mike Green. *Making Sense of Change Management: A Complete Guide to the Models, Tools and Techniques of Organizational Change.* Philadelphia, Pennsylvania: Kogan Page, 2009.

Charvet, Shelle Rose. *Words that Change Minds: Mastering the Language of Influence.* Dubuque, Iowa: Kendall/Hunt Publishing, 1997.

Dilts, Robert. *Strategies of Genius, Volume I: Aristotle, Sherlock Holmes, Walt Disney, Wolfgang Amadeus Mozart.* Capitola, California: Meta Publications, 1994.

Dinsmore, Paul C. *Human Factors in Project Management.* New York, New York: American Management Association, 1990.

Filley, Alan. *Interpersonal Conflict Resolution.* Glenview, Illinois: Scott, Foresman, 1975.

Geddes, Michael, Wendy Briner, and Colin Hastings. *Project Leadership.* Farnham, Surrey, UK: Gower, 1999.

Glaser, R., and Glaser, C. *Team Effectiveness Profile.* King of Prussia, Pennsylvania: Organization Design and Development, 1992.

Hillson, David, and Ruth Murray-Webster. *Understanding and Managing Risk Attitude.* Burlington, Vermont: Gower Publishing, 2007.

Hooper, Alan, and John Potter. *Intelligent Leadership.* New York, New York: Random House, 2001.

James, Kim Turnbull, and Tanya Arroba. "Reading and Carrying: A Framework for Learning about Emotion and Emotionality in Organizational Systems as a Core Aspect of Leadership Development." Sage Journals, 36, no. 3 (2005): 299–316.

Kozak-Holland, Mark. *Titanic: Project Management Blunders.* Lakefield, Ontario, Canada: Multi-Media Publications, 2012.

Kozak-Holland, Mark. *Titanic Lessons for IT Projects.* Lakefield, Ontario, Canada: Multi-Media Publications, 2005.

Levin, Ginger. *Interpersonal Skills for Portfolio, Program, and Project Managers.* Vienna, Virginia: Management Concepts, 2010.

Lewis, Byron, and Frank Pucelik. *Magic of NLP Demystified.* Portland, Oregon: Metamorphous Press, 1990.

Mersino, Anthony. *Emotional Intelligence for Project Managers: The People Skills You Need to Achieve Outstanding Results.* Newtown Square, Pennsylvania: Project Management Institute, 2005.

O'Connor, Joseph, and John Seymour. *Introducing NLP.* London: The Aquarian Press, 1990.

Scouller, James. *The Three Levels of Leadership: How to Develop Your Leadership Presence, Knowhow and Skill.* Management Books, 2011.

The Stationery Office (TSO). Managing Successful Projects with PRINCE2® 2009.

Tuckman, B. W. *"Developmental sequence in small groups." Psychological Bulletin* 63 (1965):384–99.

Vijay K. Verma. *The Human Aspects of Project Management: Human Resource Skills for the Project Manager, Volume 2.* Newtown Square, Pennsylvania: Project Management Institute, 1996.

Watzlawick PhD, Paul, Janet Beavin Bavelas PhD, and Don D. Jackson MD. *Pragmatics of Human Communication: A Study of Interactional Patterns, Pathologies, and Paradoxes.* New York, New York: Norton, 1967.

Welch, Jack. "The *Five Stages of Crisis Management.*" *Wall Street Journal* (New York, New York), Sept. 14, 2005.

Ziaukas, Tim. "Titanic and Public Relations: A Case Study." *Journal of Public Relations Research* 2, no. 19 (1999): 105.

Images

Figure 1 - Lord Pirrie and Bruce Ismay inspecting ship. This photograph was used courtesy of the Ulster Folk & Transport Museum

Figure 2 – Shows the ten decks, named from the bottom upwards. This image is in the public domain because its copyright has expired.

Figure 3 - The spacious drawing office at Harland and Wolff in Belfast. This photograph was used courtesy of the Ulster Folk & Transport Museum.

Figure 4 - This IMM advert is in the public domain because its copyright has expired.

Figure 5 - The *New York Times* announcement
highlighted the scale up in ships from the
current line, to the competition, to the
planned. The evolution in ship size. Courtesy
of the *New York Times* archives.

PRINCE2® is a registered trade mark of the Cabinet
Office.

Index

About the Author

Ranjit Sidhu is an experienced project and change management consultant, with more than twenty years' business experience, gained on global projects spanning Europe, North America, and Africa. During this time, she observed that however clever the processes and technology applied to projects, these alone were not enough to achieve success. Effective interaction among people, through successful communication and interpersonal skills, was critical at every stage of the life cycle. She also realized that because of the temporary nature of project teams and the speed with which they are assembled at the start of a project, it is very important for managers to understand team dynamics and fast development

of teams to get them working efficiently.

Building on her background of change and project management consultancy, Ranjit set up ChangeQuest in 2005, offering training and consultancy to help organizations improve their project and change management capability. By combining NLP, project management, and change management expertise with the latest insights from business psychology, she helps create just the right balance between focusing on the process and the people aspects of projects, so people become more effective at managing themselves and their interactions with others, and organizations can deliver change successfully and consistently.

Getting in Touch

Your comments and suggestions about this book are very welcome; please send your feedback to the e-mail address shown below.

For additional resources and articles or for ideas about developing your skills further, please visit the ChangeQuest website.

E-mail: ranjit@changequest.co.uk

Website: www.changequest.co.uk

Did you like this book?

If you enjoyed this book, you will find more interesting books at

www.MMPubs.com

Please take the time to let us know how you liked this book. Even short reviews of 2-3 sentences can be helpful and may be used in our marketing materials. If you take the time to post a review for this book on Amazon.com, let us know when the review is posted and you will receive a free audiobook or ebook from our catalog. Simply email the link to the review once it is live on Amazon.com, with your name, and your mailing address—send the email to orders@mmpubs.com with the subject line "Book Review Posted on Amazon."

If you have questions about this book, our customer loyalty program, or our review rewards program, please contact us at info@mmpubs.com.

Multi-Media Publications Inc.

Project Management Blunders: Lessons from the Project that Built, Launched, and Sank *Titanic*

White Star's initiative to build its new *Olympic*-class ships can be described as a text book project. It started off very well in the initiation and planning phases: the project team had a very good understanding of the business and customer needs, a solid vision, a superlative business case, the right supplier partnerships, good stakeholder relationships, and a healthy balance of proven and emerging technologies.

By the end of the design phase, however, decisions were made that compromised safety features. The belief in the ship's invincibility grew through the sea trials and into the maiden voyage. Everyone—from the captain and crew to the 53 millionaires on board—believed this.

This book reveals the project management blunders that doomed *Titanic* while it was still being built—mistakes that you can avoid repeating in your own projects. Filled with photos and copies of actual documents from the project, this book walks you through a case study in project management failure.

ISBN: 9781554891221   (paperback)

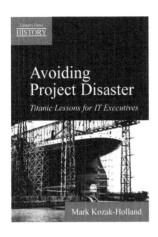

Avoiding Project Disaster: Titanic Lessons for IT Executives

Imagine you are in one of *Titanic's* lifeboats. As you look back at the wreckage, you wonder what could have happened. What were the causes? How could things have gone so badly wrong?

Titanic's maiden voyage was a disaster waiting to happen as a result of the compromises made in the project that constructed the ship. This book explores how modern executives can take lessons from a nuts-and-bolts construction project like *Titanic* and use those lessons to ensure the right approach to developing online business solutions.

Avoiding Project Disaster is about delivering IT projects in a world where being on time and on budget is not enough. You also need to be up and running around the clock for your customers and partners. This book will help you successfully maneuver through the ice floes of IT management in an industry with a notoriously high project failure rate.

ISBN: 9781895186734   (paperback)

http://www.mmpubs.com/disaster

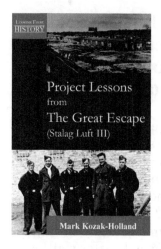

Project Lessons from The Great Escape (Stalag Luft III)

While you might think your project plan is perfect, would you bet your life on it?

In World War II, a group of 220 captured airmen did just that – they staked the lives of everyone in the camp on the success of a project to secretly build a series of tunnels out of a prison camp their captors thought was escape proof.

The prisoners formally structured their work as a project, using the project organization techniques of the day. This book analyzes their efforts using modern project management methods and the nine knowledge areas of the *Guide to the Project Management Body of Knowledge* (PMBoK).

Learn from the successes and mistakes of a project where people really put their lives on the line.

ISBN: 9781895186802   (paperback)

http://www.mmpubs.com/escape

Polaris: Lessons in Risk Management

Risk management is one of the most important practices that a manager can employ to help drive a successful outcome from a project. Good risk management allows organizations to proactively respond to risks.

Unfortunately, many managers believe risk management to be too time consuming or too complicated. Some find it to be shrouded in mystery.

This book is designed to demystify risk management, explaining introductory and advanced risk management approaches in simple language. To illustrate the risk management concepts and techniques, this book uses real-life examples from a very influential project that helped change the course of world history -- the project that designed and built the Polaris missile and accompanying submarine launch system that became a key deterrent to a Soviet nuclear attack during the Cold War. The Polaris design and construction project employed many risk management approaches, inventing one that is still widely used today.

Containing a foreword by James R. Snyder, one of the founders of the Project Management Institute (PMI), this book is structured to align with the risk management approach described in PMI's the Project Management Body of Knowledge (PMBOK Guide).

ISBN: 9781554890972   (paperback)

CPSIA information can be obtained at www.ICGtesting.com
Printed in the USA
LVOW01s1323090715

445604LV00027B/302/P

9 781554 891207